Auspicious
Good Fortune

One woman's inspirational journey
from Western disillusionment to
Eastern spiritual fulfilment

Auspicious
Good Fortune

One woman's inspirational journey
from Western disillusionment to
Eastern spiritual fulfilment

Sumangali Morhall

BOOKS

Winchester, UK
Washington, USA

First published by O-Books, 2012
O-Books is an imprint of John Hunt Publishing Ltd., Laurel House, Station Approach,
Alresford, Hants, SO24 9JH, UK
office1@o-books.net
www.o-books.com

For distributor details and how to order please visit the 'Ordering' section on our website.

Text copyright: Sumangali Morhall 2011

ISBN: 978 1 78099 036 1

A CIP catalogue record for this book is available from the British Library.

Design: Stuart Davies

Printed in the UK by CPI Antony Rowe
Printed in the USA by Edwards Brothers Malloy

We operate a distinctive and ethical publishing philosophy in all
areas of our business, from our global network of authors to
production and worldwide distribution.

CONTENTS

Introduction

When first discovering a night sky, the eyes may pick out a few tiny stars. Waiting and watching reveals thousands, until it seems there is yet more light than empty blackness. So my life has been, and so it continues. This is my story, in gratitude to Sri Chinmoy: for teaching me how to wait, and how to watch.

Revelations, no matter their size, seem to hide when they are hunted down by thoughts and wonderings. Like untamed creatures in their own private world, they only let themselves be seen when I am either still and quiet, or disarmed by helplessness. This is no new phenomenon. I dare say everyone has been struck by at least one bolt of inner brilliance while the senses are otherwise engaged in the beauty of a sunset, or the smile of a child, or the grandeur of the open sea. Ironically, sudden insights may also come when one is at a complete loss to unravel the mysteries of life, suspended somewhere in the universe on this relatively small rock, all of us together and yet so very much alone. Rather than leaving such revelations to chance, one can consciously harness and harvest them through meditation. Ultimately the moments string themselves together into a constant stream of understanding – a full and open connection to the divine.

Or so I believe. While I am yet far from reaching that exalted state, I have witnessed enough to know it exists: through increasing glimmers of my own experience, and most of all through the presence of a genuine spiritual Master.

I often wonder how I had the good fortune to find Sri Chinmoy, or even to take up any sort of spiritual practice at all. On paper it was highly unlikely, having been born into an atheist English family, and yet perhaps that very background played its own essential role. I was brought up never to leave things to chance. If something was broken, I was taught to study its components – at least in order to inform myself of how it was made, if not to mend it. I was encouraged to believe that everything could be questioned or taken apart, physically or theoretically: that everything follows logical reason, whether or not we understand the reason at a given time. Extending the theory to life in general, I always felt empowered to shape my destiny.

Although I still have faith in that empirical spirit, and in my ability to change my life for the good, I now consider a pragmatic attitude – however positive – as only part of a much wider truth. While it is no doubt vital to give one's best, it seems there is also a time to let go one's grasp, to trust in something bigger, to admit that one does not have the answers, and to be at peace with that for now.

It was at such a time when Sri Chinmoy arrived in my world. I did not think I was looking for an Indian Guru, and he was not at all as I imagined an Indian Guru to be. He was smiling and clean-shaven, as gentle as he was inconceivably strong, his childlike humour in easy balance with a wisdom that seemed older than the world itself. He was eminently practical, acutely conscious of the human condition, and yet not bound at all by the sort of petty earthliness that seemed to dog my own existence. He carried an abundance of everything I had longed for in life: constancy and creativity, freedom and sensitivity, certainty, peacefulness and most of all, immaculate poise. He brought me answers to questions I had not even yet formed: in poetry, in songs, in physical demonstration and silent meditation. He charted maps for me: maps of immediate inner lands, and others I will not reach for a very long time.

I made many mistakes before finding him; error itself had been my faithful tutor until then. I tried many apparent shortcuts to fulfilment, each of them ending in its own cul-de-sac. If nothing else, I discovered quite clearly what I do not want in life, before discovering what I do. Finding happiness through a process of elimination is, after all, a way of finding happiness – albeit a tortuous one. While I would not necessarily have chosen such a long route, I have come to realise the journey is an intrinsic part of the destination. If a pilot somehow found a way to perch a helicopter on the summit of Everest, his satisfaction and exhilaration would surely not compare to that of a mountaineer, even if they shared the same view at the end of the day.

According to Sri Chinmoy, the past is dust: we must learn from our mistakes and then continue on our way, carrying only that new knowledge with us, and leaving the useless weight of failure behind. I have come to show you the pieces of my past, not to confess my own secret hurts and imperfections – they are far from useful or exceptional – but to illustrate the extraordinary transforming influence Sri Chinmoy has had on this otherwise ordinary person: proof that the past is indeed dust, and that each of us may leave it behind if we choose.

I have neither designed nor necessarily deserved my good fortune. It came when I both needed it and was ready to accept it; when taking apart the components of my life no longer informed me well enough to mend it myself. After much racing around in pursuit of happiness, I found it had been inside me all along; I only needed to be still and quiet, knowing how and where to look. These are the real secrets I have come to tell you, in the hope of bringing that same good fortune to you, wherever you are on this relatively small rock. While we each must make our own steps to the peaks of spirituality, many have already gone before us, so we are never really alone.

There have been bleak nights along my way, many of my own making, but life is all the brighter for them now. To the human eye, without the darkness there are no stars.

3

I

Nearly the End

Each human life abides
Between the cheerful question of life,
'Who am I?'
And the powerful answer of death,
'I am all.' [1]
—Sri Chinmoy

Sun blared from a mass of windows and metal roofs. We stared forward in three lanes, hands on the wheel in the hope of a sudden advance, but it did not come. The swallows sliced through empty sky, almost too high to see, taunting us with their freedom. I sniffed through my window for a hint of breeze, but the air was as motionless as the clod of traffic to which I added. Children pressed themselves into gargoyles against other half-closed windows, or fought red-faced with one another. Adults gradually abandoned their cars to squint into the warped heat, or to lie out on the verges. Although some were happier in air-conditioning, we all shared the discomfort of not knowing how long our wait would be. There must have been an accident, so impatience seemed inappropriate. Road accidents made me especially pensive. I reflected on a question whose answer had as yet evaded me: *Who am I?*

I had dabbled in meditation for eight years, and felt sure I would never be truly happy, or truly me, unless I practised it more sincerely. Silence, stillness and solitude frightened me more than anything though. I suspected any sort of spiritual commitment would be like a colourless concrete cell, leaving me just my failings for company. I was not ready to be thus caged, and yet did not treasure life's liberty either. The cruelties and complexities of the world bewildered me such that I only sought to escape them or numb myself to them by then, thinking mine was too small a strength to stretch beyond. I travelled through that world like a television channel hopper, impulsively flicking the remote, never finding anything worth my attention, growing only more indolent and disillusioned, baffled and bored by things that seemed to be enough for most people. I was as though half alive: sufficient to function, but no longer to feel.

I could well have spent my time wondering *Who is God?* That seemed a question at once easier and more complex than the one I had chosen. While I was uncomfortable with the name and preferred not to speak it aloud, it was a tidy label for the definition I had honed in the privacy of my thoughts: ultimate love, limitless power, endless time, boundless creativity; a kindly and terrible force that I had always trusted, yet felt uncertain I could ever know or comprehend. Although God was always a *He* – only because an *It* would have been impolite and a *She* never crossed my mind – I did not subscribe to any specific image: old perhaps, but not necessarily bearded.

I assumed the only way God could wake me from my state of inner inertia would be through a serious car accident. I cannot qualify or explain that further – it was just something I carried with me from the future; the same way a scar records an event from the past. As a last resort I was sure He would take away all signs of outer beauty, and perhaps the use of my limbs, so as to soften my mischief and wastefulness. Then, I promised Him, He would have my full attention. Until then, I would hunt for shallow pleasures, instead of diving deep to where my real happiness hid.

Eventually we inched forward, sun-dazed and dozy from sitting so long on the open griddle of the road. I passed the site of the crash with more than a natural fascination or reverence.

Half spectator, half spectre, I surveyed my own potential future. One day that might be me splayed on the hot asphalt, or cut out from metal twisted up like a ball of paper, finally strapped to a stretcher in a whirr of blue lights and sirens. The sticky tyre marks, the shattered glass, the shattered limbs, would then be mine.

I knew only one prayer by heart – *The Lord's Prayer* – so I always offered it silently and superstitiously at such a scene. It was my way of telling God I still knew who was boss, that I was merely His wayward child, that no tiny will of mine could defy His – at least not indefinitely. Any time He chose, I knew He could mould me, steer me, or obliterate me, blow me like a leaf from here to Kingdom Come...

...Thy Will be done, on earth as it is in Heaven...

That was as far as I got before my own turn came. I was in the middle lane, about to overtake a slower driver, when his indicator winked towards me. I assumed he would wait for me to pass, since there was barely half a car's length between us. Probably dizzy from the heat and the chaos of children in the back seat, he failed to check his blind spot and pulled in front. As I was moving faster, the gap between us shrank to little more than a hand span. I braked and flashed a glance outwards to find the fast lane clear. Yanking my car into it and fighting hard to straighten the curve, I missed the intruder and the central reservation by inches. He drove on oblivious.

My servant of a vehicle was suddenly a hulking weapon with its own agenda, and I its hapless captive. In a far corner of memory I found that I should take my foot off the brake and steer into the swerve to regain control. I had nothing to lose and no time to question. Puffing hard, I wrenched myself from the clutch of natural instinct and shared my will with that of the machine. The traffic emptied around me, but three lanes still gave too narrow a space. The back end writhed like a fish on a hook, and the car's strength at last outbid my own.

Other cars had stopped in a straight line, like a drive-in theatre audience. I was centre-stage, turning a perfect pirouette on four wheels, seemingly in slow motion. I have not seen anything similar before or since, and I cannot say I saw it with my physical eyes even then: an ethereal body of light floating before the audience, a bright screen beyond which nobody could pass. Its form was hazy, but the light seemed people-shaped – several figures holding hands, like the paper-chain figures I used to cut out in kindergarten. They mingled with the sun's force: more powerful, more beautiful than earthly light, yet almost completely imperceptible. I had glimpsed another world that I had only hoped existed until that day. Like the flash of a deer's tail or a kingfisher's wing, it disappeared again into its own secret realm, leaving its trace only in memory.

Though I probably turned just three or four times, those tiny seconds were hours to me. I had thought until then that it was a Hollywood invention, but my life did rush before me in that blink of time. Twenty-five years of snapshots flipped in front of my mind like a film on fast-forward. Family and forgotten people, shames and errors, brilliance and victory, fond places and old belongings came tumbling as if from some giant scrapbook.

In case it was the last time we would be together, I peered down at my arms and hands redundantly holding the wheel, my legs and feet poised above the useless pedals, and thanked them for their service. *Goodbye hands*: pale hands, small fingers that learned to brush a steady line on canvas, that wrote letters of love and curious songs, that sowed dry seeds in the fragrant earth. *Goodbye feet:* little feet that loved bare sands and shady grasses, stubby toes and narrow fans of bone that bore me out of infancy and danced me into many dawns.

I cannot say I heard it with my physical ears, but I was aware of a conversation then, seemingly above and all around me, as huge as the sky. I had no idea to whom God was speaking; I felt as a child crouching at a keyhole, eavesdropping on my parents, knowing I was the subject of the exchange but unable to catch the words. All I knew was that for now I was really none of my business, and that I would have to wait quietly until a verdict was reached. There was apparently little choice.

Although I carried many petty and irrational fears at that age, in the face of death or disfigurement, I was oddly unafraid. Impatience was by far my strongest impulse in those seeming hours of spinning. The unknown was far more terrible than anything; any outcome would have been bearable if only I knew what I had to face. For almost a decade I had deliberately avoided something important, and was ready to be redirected. I resolved therefore not to sulk or to take the result as a punishment – I had accepted this day long ago. Beyond my human petulance was a thrill that God was so tangibly near, and in absolute control. In my sudden helplessness I felt only safe, like an infant in the cup of His Hand. There was love then. Only love. Inside and all around.

That string of earthly seconds seemed to stretch across a whole afternoon in Heaven's annex. Waiting. An ear pressed to a keyhole. Eventually a decision was made: one that I had assumed was not even on the list of options. The car crushed itself quite squarely from behind into the central reservation. The front half, and myself in it, remained untouched. The rest was as a soda can, flattened underfoot.

The world drifted back to normal speed, and I back into a very ordinary state of mind. I knew neither joy nor gratefulness for my reprieve; only a single-minded fury at the other driver. Opening my door without effort or obstruction, I hurtled down the middle lane of the motorway, punching my fist in the air and letting out a few choice expletives. It would have been comical to watch, but nobody felt much like laughing.

The careless driver had stopped a quarter mile ahead and was already reversing back up the hard shoulder. I was quite ready to confront him, for all the good that would have done, but luckily some members of the audience were faster runners than I was. Two surfers on their way to Cornwall reached me first, collecting me by the arms and suggesting that turning back might be for the best. Having survived the last few minutes, I had better not taunt fate by prancing down the M5 motorway. We three returned to find the rest of the audience yet more amazed by my mobility than by the whole spinning incident. The front row and much of the second came out to console or congratulate me. Some came only to convince themselves that the heat had not addled them, that I really was alive.

Despite the overflow of my adrenaline, the surfers insisted I was shocked and ought to sit quietly in their car until the police arrived. They left me with my thoughts and some cold lemonade, to recruit more help shunting the wreckage off the road. They would not let me speak to the careless driver when he came. He was obviously a decent fellow, and utterly remorseful, but they did not trust my impulses any more than I did.

The police constable had probably seen too many so-called accidents conjured by the hands of reckless youth. On a holiday weekend he would probably rather be at home with his family and a barbecue than be roasting himself by a motorway in a dark polyester uniform. For the shortened car, a misshapen barrier, and a good deal of rubber on the road, there were two possible culprits. I could not really blame him for his choice.

There was a thirty-something, leaving a wife and two curious youngsters to watch from a sober-coloured saloon. He pushed a brush of sandy hair from behind his glasses, rolled back on his heels and stuffed his hands disarmingly into the pockets of his chinos. Above the tan collar of a polo shirt his face already wore the lines of parenthood: a knowing smile knitted with a frown of concern. Had the constable allowed him a few words, he would have found him assertive and well spoken.

There was a twenty-something, with tightly folded arms –

bare to the shoulders except for a swathe of wide bangles and ribbons. Two similarly ribboned plaits danced beside a milk-white face, inlaid with two furious green-blue eyes. Her shortened vehicle had been the only one affordable that morning at her local car rental. It was a model especially popular with teenage boys, in metallic sapphire with go-faster stripes. Had the constable allowed her a few words, he would have found her tempestuous and somewhat childlike.

The constable preferred to hear from the witnesses first, recording much of the story – as told by the surfers – in a little book. I issued barely anything afterwards; uncertain the mere muscles of my mouth would contain my indignation. As the constable lectured me on hogging the middle lane and driving too close to other vehicles, the surfers took turns to interrupt, but he had already prepared his speech. When the chiding was over, all that was left was to see me to the nearest service station, where I could try to resume my journey. As to who would take me, the constable saw no choice: of course I would ride with him in the police car. I looked to the surfers, unable to face any other direction, and felt the first prickles of tears. One opened their passenger door, one picked up my salvaged bag, and we drove into the fading sun. As hopes of making last orders at their favourite Cornish pub were already disappearing with the daylight, they offered to make a detour into Bristol. We stopped at the services so I could call the person I was meeting.

'Are you crazy or just stupid?' yelped the other voice 'Even a five-year-old wouldn't take a ride from strangers!'

Against all common sense I knew I was still in the Hand of God. I glanced through the phone box window as one of them folded a wheelchair into a car for an elderly lady, and the other passed a paper-wrapped ice cream through the door behind me. They wore board shorts and sandals, all brightly dancing eyes and sunny smiles, framed by golden curls. I had met kindness, as if for the first time.

'It's okay,' I grinned into the receiver, then splitting into laughter at the lavish hints of goodness unfolding around me. 'I don't know why, but it's okay.'

It was then, as my anger dissolved, that I noticed things had changed. Everything had changed, and so radically that it was obvious only I could have changed, while everything else stayed as it had always been. The sweetness of cold air from the dashboard vents, the sparkle of lemon on my tongue, the numbing joy that only ice cream knows, the open arms of the sun as it sang the day's final phrases, the lazy beat on the radio: all were lines of some unfinished symphony. I wondered if I had ever truly seen or felt anything before.

By night I cried like a newborn, wrung out with shock and relief. Sleep was far away in some unreachable land, so I crept out onto the deck. That I could even walk brought more tears in torrents; every bone and sinew remained whole and moved in synchrony to bear me forward. I had gained a new and pristine life. Each step was hallowed, like venturing onto virgin snow.

Electric light hung in globes along the wharf and in the patches of apartment windows. It peppered the distant streets, and capered along the river's surface. It mingled in the water with reflected stars: a man-made world under the eyes of the heavens. I had noticed many scenes like it before, but had never really looked. I had heard too the chink of rigging on the masts of tethered sailing boats, but that night it was an orchestra of chimes, enchanted by the breeze. That night, though just like others past, held the most beauty I had ever witnessed.

A lone church bell told midnight. It was Sri Chinmoy's birthday, August twenty-seventh: soon to become my favourite day of every year. That auspicious fact, unknown to me then, was just one snippet in the paper trail of my fortune.

2

Leaves and Leaving

Each child
Is a new wonder.
Each child
Is a new discoverer.
Each child
Is an ever-new dawn-harbinger. [2]
—Sri Chinmoy

It is said that a soul, with the guidance of God, chooses to enter a particular family for particular reasons: chasing strands of karma woven through prior lives, or matching traits of character and vocation, all in pursuit of its own development. If any of my close relations had believed in such things as God and souls, they might have put my arrival down to an administrative error. They accepted it in good spirit either way.

I was born in Sussex at the start of the seventies, to a family of mechanical engineers. My grandfather, father and mother, later my stepfather and only sibling, all founded their careers on engineering genes: genes that by some freak of science I did not inherit. I arrived equipped with other more nebulous qualities. An enigma, a source of amusement and curiosity, I became the secret object of their fondness. Like a mascot of a different species in an otherwise orderly regiment, I was the exception that proved the rule. My mother tried to take the blame for my peculiarity: she claimed it was due to her reading *The Lord of the Rings* while still carrying me. Had she known, she would have chosen a more pedestrian book, but after a few pages Tolkien is not so easy to put down. That and craving too many plums she was sure accounted for it all.

Technically I was an accident. Probably many children are, but not all are blessed with candid parents. I had obviously been accepted anyway, and that was what mattered. From the day they saw me into the world, I was their 'little friend'; they spoke to me as an adult from the start, long before I could shape any words for myself. I listened intensely and only repeated anything when I knew I had it pat. My own name was the one notable compromise; its sequence of sounds evaded me. I was Sarah. When I was old enough to choose, I went by my middle name, Emily, as it seemed to fit more comfortably.

Some would claim I was nameless anyway, not having been baptised. My parents chose not to thrust religion on me; spirituality was not even open for discussion. They did not subscribe to it anyway, and spiritual choices were considered too personal to be made by anyone except the self. God was a taboo subject – it was a matter of courtesy not to bring Him into anything, like the birds and the bees. It therefore took me a while to find Him.

When I turned two, my mother told me she would soon have a new baby. I was inconsolable. Jealousy would have been natural if I thought a stranger would join our team and usurp my parents' attention, but that was not the problem: I assumed they were getting somebody to replace me, rather than to accompany me. I was horrified to think I had displeased them so badly as to warrant complete rejection, and terrified of where I would be sent, perhaps merely to be thrown out with the rubbish. Beneath my shuddering wails I finally understood I would have a 'little friend' to play with. I was grateful just to be kept – sharing parents was nothing against the idea of losing them altogether.

When my brother arrived, I was given a small soft bear to offer him in welcome. He was rolled up in so many clothes I had trouble believing he was a proper person, let alone one who might know any games. I levered the bear respectfully through the railings of his cot, one leg at a time, but he did not say thank you, or even look at me. While I was disappointed by his manners, my parents seemed so pleased with him I decided not to mention it. I had yet to learn the happy fact that we are not born as finished products.

Our ordinary English life met an abrupt end, as my father took a job in America. We followed him ten weeks after my brother was born. It was a staggered new beginning, spanning several months and various brief abodes.

Our first real home abroad was nestled in the mountain foothills behind Los Angeles. The city teemed below in its dirt and danger, but even at night it was a benign fairy-world to me: ant-sized vehicles weaving a soft glitter of red and gold around the stubs of buildings. The air was hot and clean, and everything grew avidly on our garden terraces. Gangs of coyotes sang from the mountains after dark, and sometimes from the garden. It was not the spooky, desolate sound the movies make of it. Although I never saw them, to my mind they were just a family of musical, mischievous nomads. In summer nights the mountain grass, impassioned by the wind, would ignite itself and fly into a blaze. I heard the crackle of it and saw the wide smudge of flame behind the curtains, but my father said it could not come close. My father was invincible and omniscient, so his word was enough to let me roll back to sleep.

Nobody could protect me in the more subtle realms of night though. From birth I was haunted by nightmares. Reincarnation is now my only explanation for thoughts and dreams so at odds with my protected life – a child would not imagine the things I saw inside, having never been exposed to the horrors of the world. My first dream in colour was of death, the red blood from a dying creature seeping fast into surrounding greys. I dreaded to be in a room alone, even in daylight; there seemed a sinister presence near me that I felt powerless to fight. I never told anyone. I thought they would laugh, and was too proud to admit my cowardice. The dreams could not be hidden though – I could not bear them myself, and often roused the family with imperative screams. In the half-waking haze that followed, I saw only a looming shape approaching. The parent running to my rescue was just a new shadow, and I shrieked my peril all the louder as it closed in on me.

'Think beautiful thoughts, or have no thoughts at all. Think of the sky,' counselled my mother when I asked her how to sleep again.

Shaping my own imagination into a tool, instead of letting it wield new terror against me, I took my first step into the sanctum of meditation. My efforts were strained as I unfurled the fears one by one, only to find them coiled back again: one benign creation after another, crushed by the same mind that made it. I knew there was some greater strength than this, only I could not recall it.

'But what comes after the sky? And after Space? What happens to people when they die?'

'I don't know. Probably nothing.'

'Would Daddy know?'

'No, nobody knows.'

Nobody knows. Not even Daddy. I would not believe it. It was surely a ruse to deflect my attention from just another grownup secret, like watching *Monty Python's Flying Circus*, or drinking beer, or writing a cheque. The answer was resolute and unchangeable, open neither to negotiation nor interrogation. The dawning fact that nobody did actually know was disturbing in itself; more disturbing was the fact that nobody seemed concerned. 'Nothing' was not good enough and I knew there was more. Although only a minor sleuth, I would catch that Something or Someone unawares. The adults had more secrets than I had realised, so I would simply have my own.

Telephone calls abroad came at royal prices, and sometimes had to be booked in advance. I only remember speaking to my grandparents in England once or twice; it was a muddle of delays and interruptions. The rest of the time we recorded a cassette and sent it by airmail. A new tape was posted back, with my grandmother's high warble and my grandfather's stiff growl.

'Say hello to Nanny.'

'Hello, Nannyyy,' I opened at the first attempt, edging right up to the chunky recorder and making it buzz. She did not respond, even after a suitable delay.

'There's nobody there.'

'Nanny can hear you; it's just that you can't hear *her*. Say thank you for the blouse she sent for your birthday.'

'Thank you for the blouse you sent for my birthday.' I listened closely just in case, but received only the sound of turning spools. My mother adjusted me gently away from the microphone. She smiled and nodded, raising her eyebrows encouragingly. I believed her, but it was difficult to know what to say into a void.

'Tell her the blouse is nice and cool.'

'The blouse is nice. And cool.'

'Tell her about the humming birds.' She knew that would animate me.

'Nanny, the humming birds come and drink the drink! We fill their feeder up with red drink because they like red. Their beaks are long and go right inside, and they're very small and green and shiny and their wings go so fast you nearly can't see them. That's what makes them hum. Like bees.'

Suddenly I understood. The cassette formed a sort of clue; a sign that people could potentially still be there, even if they were not seen or heard with the ordinary senses.

* * *

After another transitory apartment, our next proper home was in a corner of the Houston suburbs. The air was thick and greasy, peopled by mosquitoes and various more vulgar insects.

Compared to California, nature looked moon-barren, even in domestic gardens. It seemed there would be only two seasons: sultry and gloomy or chilled and gloomy. Everything was big but empty, so I felt hollow too. Apparently we were 'rich', which seemed to mean outwardly comfortable, but uneasy on the inside.

For the first time ever, one room was all mine. It was fit for a child princess, but it was much too alone for me. Since he was born, I had shared with my brother, so I was not ready for his absence, especially at night. His breathing and fidgeting had always diluted the darkness until then. I had all the latest toys, and a canopy bed. It was probably all I could have wished for, but to me it was just echoey and strange. What troubled me most was that my mother was not happy, and I could therefore not be happy either. I sensed a gathering darkness around her that I did not understand. Although she bore it and fought to conceal it, I silently added it to my own. We were as twin clouds merging in a storm.

Our favourite room was all for music. Its windows were the only ones not shadowed by tall pines, so it caught whatever sun could muscle through the clouds, and it led from the lobby, so no comings or goings could be missed from inside it. The day a piano arrived for my mother was one of the happiest that house ever saw. She played easily because she could read. I watched her fingers spanning chords or rippling with the flurries marked out on a page, and yearned to learn that magic from her. Music formed an arcane world to which I knew I belonged. I wanted to make those sounds much sooner than immediately, so study seemed an unbearable fee; surely it was my right to make them, only my fingers had forgotten how. It was strange and galling, but my mother's iron patience bridged the gap in my own, leading me much further than I would have managed otherwise. When I was first able to read – even the simplest and clumsiest tunes – I met with delirious joy. Each primitive victory led me on to the next.

In the creeping doom before autumn term, my mother and I squeezed out the last drops of summer at a craft fair. I lost my dread of school entirely in the trestles of knittables and nicknacks, beads, basketry and raw clay. The smells of paints and new brushes, fat yarns and waiting canvas were to me the fragrances of hope and possibility. It was a finished wooden horse who won my special favour, and I was allowed to take him home. He was my new measure of perfection, painted in white and primaries, a braid for a bridle and a bunched red mane of wool. Entranced by his beauty I trotted to the car beside my mother, turning his glossy body in my hands, and wondering what to use as a stable.

The horse's sovereignty was short-lived. Beyond him someone had dashed a fresh leaf with red paint and left it on the ground. Such adornment of nature baffled me and I crouched to collect it. Close up, the colours were outrageous – ludicrous even – not stopping at ochre or bronze or anything nearly so bland, but only crimson and scarlet and ruby, carousing on a ground of impossibly vigorous green.

'Mummy, why did someone paint it?'

'Nobody did, it fell like that.'

I pointed to an obvious blot from a brush. 'No it's red paint, look.'

Holding it out as proof, cool and damp on the flat of my hand, the truth seeped into me. Its tiny red corpuscles glowed against the green, flowing on into wide arteries and rounded reservoirs. In places the 'paint' had dribbled and spattered, but reversing it or holding it to the sky showed the colour as intrinsic. The realisation was dizzying: I had received another sly wink from the divine.

'Shall we take it home?' I asked reverently, the stunned witness of a miracle.

'Let's choose a few, they'll all be different.'

I raised my eyes to another miniature canvas on the path ahead, a cluster more, and then a broad carpet of them, all scattered in fun by the Creator. On the maple above, thousands were pinned out to dry.

There You are! I smiled in silence. Though I did not see the Painter, I knew He must be in there.

* * *

I was not a healthy child. It was a time of impromptu nosebleeds and baleful ear infections, leading to public embarrassment and cancelled social engagements. Once so nervous of making the right impression at dinner with my father's friends, I only vomited an impressive amount of green bile across the table in the process. My one attempt at summer camp saw me locked in the nurse's hut on arrival, delirious with fever. While others rode horses and learned archery and swam in the lake, I was retracted by my father and whisked to hospital in my pyjamas. Almost anything except my own society proved disastrous and humiliating, yet I dreaded being alone. I longed to be invisible, but always somehow stood out like a traffic-cone while the world hurtled by me.

My aloneness was most acute at school: a place where other people understood one another, where they knew the same games and played together easily. What I lacked in social development I invested in my study. Outgrowing some of the lessons for my age, I was promoted to the year above. Although it should have been an honour, I was frightened silly of the sassy and unpredictable older ones. I was the small and pale one, the one with the strange accent and the solemn frown, saddled and steered by my own shyness.

My closeness to my mother contrasted ever more plainly with a growing distance from my father. Instead of running to greet him after his extended trips, I only stubbornly avoided him. The faraway stories, the mysterious scents of spice and cigar smoke from his discarded jacket, were not sufficient to rouse me from the grief that had grown out of his absence. Although they were undoubtedly essential journeys that he himself would rather not have made, at that age I was the centre of my universe, and thus could only take his absence personally. From the low vantage of my childly mind, it seemed my protector had only abandoned his post again, and his return was a pale apology. I could not excuse his solo adventures as an economic necessity, and my forgiveness could not be bought for the price of an airport gift.

Families are broken by many means. Ours was more a widening fracture. My parents had initially planned a short stay abroad, then to return to England with enough finance for a family bookshop. The means instead became the end. Perhaps they married before they had properly grown into themselves and found out what it was they wanted. I would not understand that until I reached their age. As it was, a passion for wealth and society gradually engulfed my father's world, until it seemed we were no longer coupled to it.

My mother went ahead with the two of us to England, leaving my father behind, hoping thus to remind him of their lost dreams. I did not say goodbye, somehow believing I would see him in a matter of days. We would all retire then to our homeland for a shiny new beginning. The days instead clustered into months, and the phone calls spread thinner. Ultimately it was clear to me: we had become a three-man team. My father was gone from our daily lives forever, and I felt my own life was all but over. I was seven years old.

* * *

English culture posed many mysteries, and required more equipment than I was used to. Everything was a complex under-taking, but the ceremony and structure brought a kind of sombre consolation. The table wore a crisp white cloth; the chairs wore lace antimacassars; Granddad wore a tie, although he was retired. The sugar bowl – sporting a picture of the Queen – had tongs instead of a spoon. The jam was made at home with sieves and saucepans and a long thermometer. There were special sorts of forks and knives for cakes or fish that lived in their own satin-lined cases under the sideboard. Other sets of things lived there – mostly silver and crystal – that were not meant for using at all.

Granddad was stern to a fault; he considered it his role. Nanny, as if to redress, only ever indulged us. Perhaps it was that combination which prevented fear from entering their house. Not even nightmares followed me there, and darkness itself was not entirely hostile. At night I could barely move my legs under the tightness of the sheets and the weight of the eiderdown. In the next bed, my brother was close enough to reach with one hand, and to be heard in whispers. We were read a chapter from *The Waterbabies,* or something else with elderly words and morals, illustrated with etchings. Nanny then stroked my head to bring the sleep into it, but I stayed awake in secret to be near her, until she mistook my peaceful smile for slumber. She left us a sliver of light in the doorway, then to potter with her chores in other rooms, humming songs from wartime. In the mornings a soft monotony of pigeons would wake me, and the smell of baking bread.

My mother was suddenly both parents in one. She easily found a job as an engineer with a firm in Brighton. In those days women did not generally work for firms of engineers, unless they were taking notes or making the tea. God alone knows what brunt of prejudice she fended daily, but she was herself again, so enthusiasm carried her, as did her motto: *Well you just get on with it, don't you.*

We bought an *Austin 1100* for four hundred pounds. It felt like a toy compared to our American cars, but it gave the final touch to our independence. It was older than me, and painted in the particular pale blue used mostly for invalid carriages. Its furnishings were crackled like a crusty loaf, and its face was friendly. We welcomed it into the family, and respected it as an elder. Once a wheel fell off while my mother was commuting, but as the car's maximum speed was only about sixty miles per hour, nobody was hurt. She had a man mend the axel and put the wheel back on, then the car 'just got on with it' too.

As we had an income, we resolved to move from my grandparents' bungalow. Perfect for two seniors, it strained to contain a growing family of five. The brace of my grandfather's flinty routines and fossilised morals, lined with the softness of my grandmother's affection, had made us a cradle in which to find our breath. Although it was a wrench to leave their haven, having spent most of my life half a world away from them, the two-mile gap seemed bridgeable.

That was when the world began to crumble, and the truth seeped in. Finding a car without my father was one thing, but finding a home seemed unnervingly permanent. My mother was driving when she first mentioned the word 'divorce'. I never imagined something so terminal invading my own life. It sounded dirty and pitiful, like a disease discussed by adults in lowered voices. I buried it somewhere. There was nothing more I could do.

My brother and I started school in Burgess Hill, a commuting town on the route to London. It was our first encounter with uniforms. I mostly wrestled with the new layers by myself: the itchy tights, the thermal vest, the stiff-collared shirt, pleated skirt and cardigan. A uniform was exciting and grown up. It was also a sign of belonging. The tie was a step too far though, especially for my brother who was still in Infants. A little afraid of what Granddad would say if I could not do it nicely, I practised tying mine over my nightie before bed. I was in Juniors, so I did not have my brother's excuse.

I discovered there had been friends in America after all: they were neighbours, sisters of my brother's friends, daughters of my father's colleagues; each of whom I thought did not count. Having to start again I realised how much even that narrow and unearned society had meant to me. American children were sunny and exuberant; their confidence included others implicitly. Disguised in my school uniform, I should at least be able to dissolve in a crowd. That was some comfort. Since first leaving for America I had deliberately clung to my Sussex accent, and for once it fitted my environment. Maybe they would not notice I was new.

Assembly was the first part of the day. I found that it mostly involved sitting cross-legged on the floor for listening and singing, both of which I was quite good at. I did not know what a hymn was, but it seemed to be about God. I did not know God either, but apparently everyone else did, and they sang to Him from orange books with plastic jackets. Just the open pages brought me a new surge of nausea; I was more alone in that sea of voices than anywhere I had ever been. My tears clapped down on the front cover, gathering into fluid orange globes.

That was how I first learned the name of the Someone I had been tracking: I listened and did not sing. It was not a happy find, but only the start of a new confusion. Why did people just sing to Him and not talk about Him? It was not even proper singing anyway – I fancied I could give a more convincing verse of *Yellow Submarine*. *Onward Christian soldiers, marching as to war* sounded like an amble to the corner shop for milk. *Fight the good fight with all thy might* was as limp as a nursery rhyme. I would not ask my mother about it; probably 'nobody' knew. I had a sneaking fear that maybe God was like Father Christmas: a myth people were expected to grow out of. I had never subscribed to Father Christmas, and I was fairly sure God was bigger, but there was nobody to ask. The mystery had taken a worrying turn, and I was very good at worrying.

The other children wanted to dislike me at first. No doubt

seeing my bleakness, the teacher blessed me with extra attention, praising my neatness, diligence and creativity. That only seemed to make things worse. Some of the louder and more restless girls took exception, and tried to rib me for it, criticising the care I took in washing my hands and straightening my tie. I stayed silent and tried to take their comments as compliments. It was the first time I had encountered even an attempt at bullying, and it mystified me. Why would anyone want another person to feel even smaller and less happy than she already did?

My mother soon secured a mortgage on a sixteen-thousand-pound house. It was brand new – in fact not even properly finished – when we moved in. The clarity and hopefulness inside made the breath catch in my chest. We were all more thrilled than we could bear. To my particular relief there was not even space for us to live separately; my mother would have one room and I would share bunks with my brother in the next. It was the most perfect house I could have wished for.

We had everything we needed, but as for luxuries, 'going without' was something we had all grown used to. There was rarely meat for dinner anymore because it cost too much. I never liked it anyway – the texture and the smell of the red sort usually made me retch unless it was disguised, or unless it was bacon. My father always had me clear my plate, so I sometimes used to hide my meat in a napkin. My mother probably knew, but she was never keen on meat either, and would never force me. In England we had cheap and easy things that were much more palatable anyway – mainly tinned spaghetti, crispy noodles, or frozen pizzas. The only time we ate out was when my mother won the football pools at work: a dazzling sum of twenty-five pounds. Determined it would not just dissolve into the house-keeping, she took us for a chicken curry and then to the cinema, with sweets and fizzy drinks. We all wore our best things.

* * *

In spring we were each asked to bring in an empty ice cream tub to school, half filling it with weedy grey water from the nearby pond. The teacher doled out spoonfuls of transparent pond-slime, that we were to observe at home. Even close up it was disappointing: only a mass of turgid globs, each looking out from a central black eye. Why was a small jar not sufficient housing anyway? The tub stayed at our kitchen window, visited only briefly during washing-up. The black eyes grew a little at a time, and eventually started to writhe. Our cat was more attentive than anyone. I found her fixed to the ledge one morning, leaning back in an unblinking trance, one mitten twitching at the water. A black lozenge with a tail was busy evading her claws.

There You are! I thought, as I hoisted her away. Who would have believed it? God – as I then knew Him – had lived in a plastic tub by our kitchen window all along. In time He grew brown webbed fingers and muscular thighs, with which to climb from the surface. Sadly that was when the cat ate Him: when He was a nearly-frog. We thought it best to release all His remaining living forms back into the pond before He was mistaken for more snacks. I was sure again: it could not be a myth. Nobody ever saw Father Christmas, but God had displayed Himself in front of us all, right there in our house. One day He was a piece of slime, and gradually a real frog, or near enough. What more proof could anyone need? Was that not worth singing properly for? I did not say anything, but from then on I certainly opened my hymnbook during assembly. I even joined the after-school choir.

As I had entered school in the third year, French lessons were compulsory. The teacher's methods were driven by a shocking temper, which I found far from inspiring. My mother practised with me at home and made it into a game; with useful sentences, not the silly sort they put in my textbook. Other children were not so lucky, and frequently cried or wet themselves during the weekly tests. I liked learning, but the threat of a late summer field trip to France – a source of glee for everyone else – pulled at my nerves. I would be away from my mother for almost a week.

Whatever her motivation, our teacher made sure it was not a holiday. We went by ferry and coach straight into the Somme Valley: the site of one of the bloodiest battles ever. It had witnessed in one day alone nearly sixty thousand British casualties, and the only way we could be forced into gratitude for that was apparently by having our minds saturated with grisly details of the First World War. It was a relentless barrage on our unsuspecting hearts: tours of battlefields, graveyards and monuments, day after withering day. We filed through the trenches, still marked out with sandbags. Poppies bowed their heads respectfully in the surrounding fields, and the skylarks trilled a breathless elegy. The surface of every memorial looked filigreed from afar, but close up the detail was a list of a thousand more inscriptions. The graveyards were nothing like the little ones I had seen in the grounds of village churches; they stretched across acres and rolled over the horizon. In places the markers carried four names: one on each arm of the cross, and two mirrored on the back. Of course they were not only British – as if we were some unfortunate, victimised race – but the sons of twenty-four other nations too, lying together peacefully only after their lives were gone.

I was sickened enough by the British deaths, but the discovery that we were also killers was far too appalling. The total loss was more sadness than anyone could hold in at once, much less a nine-year-old child. There was no armour to my senses, and no way to separate myself from all those other selves. They were all me: shot and burned and blown apart, bloodied and buried, lost and mourned and yearned for by countless other selves. It was undoubtedly an education. From then on I knew for sure that the horror in my dreams since birth could actually happen in the outside world: it already had, and on a dreadful scale. At home everything was the same as before, but I was different – something inside had toppled and could not be put right.

3

Old York

Childhood sings
The songs of strange curiosity.
Adolescence sings
The songs of blind carelessness.
Youth sings
The songs of cold indifference.
Maturity sings
The songs of deepening nostalgia.
Dotage sings
The songs of orphan helplessness. [3]
—Sri Chinmoy

My mother started seeing someone from work: someone from Up North. We met him when he came to take her for dinner. While my brother and I were ostensibly watching science fiction in our pyjamas, drinking Nanny's milky cocoa, curiosity really had our full attention. She smiled and wore perfume; he spoke with a Yorkshire accent, smoked cigarettes from a flat foil box, and drove her away in a car called a *Princess*. He was older than she was, and very kind to her: actually almost impossibly decent, because even Granddad decided to like him straight away. I liked him too for the first few months, until I realised he wanted to marry my mother. I was wary at best after that.

Our first year passed almost without incident. The man drove us Up North in his *Princess* for Easter, where we four rented a cottage. Yorkshire was magical in spring. The heathered moorland was the first place I had ever been where there was neither dwelling nor person in sight, nor any sound. The sky was bigger than anywhere, the rocks nosing out of the scrub were grey and serious, and the shadows were longer than at home. It was humbling and it made me brood, but I liked it. There were no fences, just a few walls made of rough stones that fitted together without cement. The sheep could go wherever they pleased – we had to stop and let them cross the road. They camped on the village greens and verges, so the grass was nibbled down evenly like the pile of velvet. One entire valley was carpeted in golden stars: a cache of daffodils in wild profusion. We sat with them for a long time, and then walked on the tracks where the grass showed through. They nodded shyly and averted their gaze, watching the ground or the sparkle of a brook as it chuckled below.

All the same things happened the following Easter, only that time we were looking for a home together. My new stepfather needed to work Up North, and my mother still longed for a shop. She said it need not be a bookshop – a corner shop might be fun – and it may as well be in Yorkshire. I was determined to dislike Up North from then on, but we moved to a large village outside York in autumn anyway. Not wanting to steal my mother's happiness, I did not say anything, but made my point as best I could with silence and sulking. I was eleven, so there was nothing more I could do.

Our new home looked like it had narrowly survived a brunt of hatred from its previous owners. The woodwork had paint thrown at it in a spite of violet or pink; the walls were asphyxial yellow from nicotine. Names were carved into windowsills and the carpets were more thrashed than trodden. Without human umpire, trees and more mysterious plants were left to throttle one another in the grounds outside. The adjoining shop had been forcibly closed by the authorities, for failing to meet the basic rules of health. Every packet of every type of food was drilled through in several places by weevils. The pests invited themselves to join us in the house, but I suppose they left or starved eventually, as things were kept in tins from then on.

I started secondary school straight away. Even the thought of it brought a pain in my stomach that nearly folded me in two each morning. Perhaps my mother was concerned that I would stand out from other pupils because of my southern accent, so in a tender attempt to compensate, she followed the uniform guidelines to the letter. I had flat shoes with buckles, an A-line skirt exactly two inches below the knee, and a shirt with a top button that fastened down to accommodate a tie, like in Juniors. I was already conspicuous at the bus stop – apparently people did not set much store by uniform guidelines. Girls arrived first in angry pairs, taking double the number of normal steps because their skirts were so short and narrow. The boys gathered one by one into a cloud of smells and noise that oozed into the road, making the cars veer outwards. A few had ties showing in the vague region of their necks, but most had them wrapped around a wrist or shoved in a bag.

Hidden in the forests at a nearby brewing town, the school had been considered prestigious in its sixteenth century heyday. It still carried the label of Grammar School – a name that had mostly died out in my parents' time – meaning a place for people who had done well in their exams, but could not afford a private school. In my day, Grammar was an absurd and meaningless decoration. It was in truth a Comprehensive: a huge stockpot of mismatched odds and ends.

I did not make any friends, but equally I was left alone – at least behind the doors of a classroom. In the corridors or stairwells we first-years were routinely shoved for sport, which caused more a jolt to the nerves and confidence than any pain. I learned undignified ways to edge onto the bus every morning, securing myself one of the safer seats: nearest the driver, furthest from the jeering and swearing and surreptitious smoking at the back. The school itself also had zones where certain types of people congregated. I plotted out the most perilous areas in my mind and avoided them as best I could, or marched quickly if I must pass through, lowering my head and sometimes sneakily attaching myself to the back of a more benign group.

I dreaded break times. There were several benches by the lawns and gardens, but it was safer to stay mobile than to settle in one place. Mostly people 'walked round' following a set route, either clockwise or anti-clockwise, on the outside of the buildings. I walked round alone, which was not advisable. The worst of it was usually being spat at: a common hazard anywhere in the grounds. Even in the lavatory stalls, the older girls would stand on a neighbouring pedestal to lean over and spit, throw soaking wads of paper, or just watch and offer abuse. Once in such a vulnerable position, there was no dodging any of it. I dredged my psyche for a way to react, and came up with nothing, so I simply learned not to drink very much until I got home.

Games lessons were fairly gruesome, especially in winter. I was already a fussy eater, but the new pains in my stomach made meals a chore, leaving me increasingly thinner and weaker. I spent most of hockey or lacrosse trying to avoid the ball instead of chasing it; everything already hurt in the biting cold, so the thought of being hit or even jostled did not appeal. Showers were more dreadful than any game, and seemed pointless since I never broke a sweat. I was so much thinner without clothes, the water was sparse and lukewarm, the soap seemed composed of only industrial chemicals and the drains below were full of wet mud, so I always came out feeling colder and dirtier than before. The worst was forgetting a towel or a piece of kit, and having to borrow from Lost Property, where everything was itchy and smelled of feet.

The advantage of despising school was that I loved my new home more. The house was still a disaster, but our corner shop was ready to reopen within a few weeks. I first assumed living

Up North would mean remaining cold, squashed and spat upon forever more, but the shop became a source of life and hope for all of us. It was a beacon of colourful welcome in the long winter evenings. Although the fittings and fridges were decrepit, they were scrubbed clean, full to bursting with everything from the barest essentials to comparative luxuries. The back wall was taken up entirely by heavy jars of sweets, to be scooped into paper bags and sold by the quarter-pound: bonbons and sherbet powder, toffees and gums, jellies and chocolates and mints – some in little pips, glossy balls, or cubes twisted into foil. Under them were trays of penny chews and oily strands of liquorice.

My stepfather worked constantly. When he was not in the office at his engineering job or serving customers, he was in a big white boiler suit: breaking down boxes, mopping something, mending something or painting something else. I would sit at the back of the shop with my homework after school, while my mother saw to a constant stream of gossiping neighbours. It amused me that gangs of older kids who would never normally dream of speaking to me, came into part of my home to buy cigarettes, or hung around outside on our forecourt with their battered cars, showing off to other gangs of kids. Ironically our house was suddenly the place to be seen.

We were open seven days, including evenings. There was help on Saturdays so my mother could have a day off, half of which she spent making us a roast dinner. On Sundays I worked with her all day, which made me feel very important, if not indispensable. My duties were restocking from the little storeroom, especially the sweets as they sold the fastest. I became expert at wrapping loaves or bottles in sheets of tissue for the customers, and cutting them cheese from big blocks using a wire. We sold sherry by the pint from barrels, which I was allowed to funnel into any containers people brought from home. Shop work absorbed me completely, and left me happier than any other pastime.

* * *

In the second year of school, I sat with a girl called Laura, who liked to be known as Squid. I never discovered why – it was something her family called her and she liked it. She wore lots of beaded jewellery under her shirt so the teachers would not see, but rolled back her cuffs and loosened her tie whenever they were not around. Her hair was rusty orange and sprayed out in spikes at the front. She had a big scar in her cheek: something to do with a tin of baby food. It had apparently been a small scar to start with, but had grown with her, eventually making her look somewhat menacing from the side. She wore short leather ankle boots with very obvious seams, and made sure to tell me it was humanely produced leather from a certain shop in London.

Squid liked to talk, and I liked to listen, so we became friends straight away. As far as she was concerned, lessons were unfortunate distractions from a lot of very important things happening in the outside world, which she imparted to me in grim detail. Sometimes she even went on demonstrations about them with her mother, which was apparently very daring and dangerous. They held placards with lots of other people and shouted about a particular issue in the street. It made the farmers angry and usually the police as well. I thought it sounded grownup but unappealing, like something on the news.

Squid's two pet hates were vivisection and war, so every day she brought me new photographs of animal experiments or evidence of weapons being developed by various countries. My genuine horror and concern inspired her to add pictures of poultry farms and slaughterhouses as well, with accompanying stories. There was a cow just before being stunned, with its eyes half white in terror. There were chickens with their beaks clipped off, or doomed to perpetual darkness, existing for years in wire cubicles no bigger than their own bodies. The flayed carcasses were the worst; they made the connection between a live animal and a piece of meat abundantly clear.

'Everybody eats meat though,' I countered, 'does it all come from places like this?'

'You think it grows on trees?'

'What if people don't ever eat meat though? Won't they die?'

'I haven't eaten meat since I was five. Do I look dead? I'm a *vegetarian*.'

The word was defiant and absolute. I knew from that moment that I was a vegetarian too. Suddenly it made perfect sense that I had never liked meat; meat was just a dead body, why would I want to put that in my mouth? Anyway, if I could live without causing suffering to another living being, especially one so helpless as an animal, then why would I deliberately continue such a strange practice? It seemed hypocritical to keep a cat as a pet and meanwhile cause the deaths of other animals for food. To her credit my mother did not even flinch when I told her, but did wonder what on earth to feed a vegetarian who did not like vegetables. At least she knew what a vegetarian was. She also knew they were a rare breed at the time and required particular care: presumably very special care if they were already thin and trying to grow. The next day was Saturday, so we would find a health food shop and get some proper advice. Being a traditional meat-and-two-veg Yorkshireman, my stepfather delighted in poking fun, and so did my brother, but my mother hushed them both for me. For the first time ever, I did not care what they thought, even though apparently they thought I was being impetuous and impressionable. They probably also assumed I would grow out of it.

As for the sudden issue of war, I already had a belly full of that in France, but Squid made sure I understood a war on that scale would be indescribably worse in our time. Whole cities or countries could be obliterated at the push of a button; not just armed soldiers out in the countryside, but every single man, woman, child, animal and building. She said even if it did not come to the use of atomic weapons, women might be conscripted as well as men. That was too much. I had gained not one new friend but two: Squid and insomnia. They were inseparable. The familiar sinister presence had not subsided with my increase in age by any means, and neither had the nightmares. They suddenly had much more imagery to feed on: real horrors, not only imaginary ones. My fear felt entirely justified, and therefore sat more firmly on my shoulders. In the small hours of the night, everything became unbearably vivid: a Hiroshima mushroom cloud, the resulting desolation, children burning and screaming or lying dead with their faces blown off, others barely surviving the following cold and sickness, surrounded by only gruesome deaths. I could not separate myself from all those people, and I thought it would be callous to try. By night, every one of them was me.

At school – our microcosm of the world – fighting was a daily ritual. There were often impromptu 'scraps' between two boys, or two girls. They would draw instant crowds from anyone nearby, and others came from out of sight when the bloodthirsty chant rose up: *Scrap! Scrap! Scrap! Scrap!* Sometimes a fight would be scheduled in advance between two willing partici-pants, and a broadcast would spread by word of mouth with a time and location. If the plan did not reach the teachers' ears it would draw a larger crowd, and was thus harder to defuse, especially when big names were billed to compete. Other times a challenger would announce that he or she was going after a particular person on a particular day: prompted by an insult, or just out of boredom. The victim would then need to be hunted down by the challenger's gang, so the details were more sponta-neous. If he was found but was not up to fighting, he would be beaten up anyway: sometimes by the whole gang. The worst scraps were between groups: maybe year three against year four, or one class against another. Sometimes hundreds joined in on the playing fields, and hundreds more turned up to watch. In the mass fights there were missiles: whatever anyone could get their hands on, like bricks, stones, or nails and pieces of timber stolen from the woodwork rooms. The worst of the troublemakers had usually just been released from reform school, and were sent straight back there if they were caught injuring anyone. Usually there were as many being released as there were being sent back though, so there was always a quorum of aggressors.

Towards the end of spring term, a new girl called Amanda arrived in a long black trench coat. Squid was much enamoured of her because she knew a lot about war, and had also been on demonstrations. Amanda tolerated my presence, even though I had never been arrested and was not a member of any liberation societies. The three of us walked round together at lunchtimes, and shared a bunsen burner in chemistry, but there was something odd about Amanda. It was as if she was not quite plugged in properly.

At the start of summer term, Squid and Amanda had apparently spent a lot of time together in the holidays. As they marched into the classroom, wearing each other's earrings, Amanda was the first to greet me.

'Oh look, it's Mole. We're calling you Mole. It's your new name, so you have to answer to it. Say something, Mole.'

Unable to translate that into anything worth a response, I just stared down at my shoes. They were pale blue lace-ups in leather as soft as rosebuds.

'New shoes Mole, they look a bit clean. We can help you with that, because we're your friends.'

Amanda was already clamping my arms behind me, and dragging me backwards out of my chair onto the floor. Other girls looked away to continue their chatter, propped or perched on the edges of desks. The boys whooped and leered as Squid dug her thumbs into my ankles and wrenched off the shoes without untying them, so they bruised along the bridges of my feet.

'What shall we do with them, Mole?'

It seemed she had already decided, as she was dangling them out of the window by their laces.

'Oops.'

They were gone. I snatched my arms away from Amanda, who was laughing so hard she had lost most of her strength. Red-faced and numb with confusion, I bolted down seemingly endless stairs, and out onto the damp lawn in my socks. At least nobody had got to them before me. The pale blue was defiled with grass cuttings and mud, but that was the least of my new troubles. Assembly dredged up the familiar feeling from Juniors, only I was sitting on wooden terraces instead of the floor. Across the plasticised cover of my hymnbook, tears gathered into liquid purple globes rather than orange.

At break time Squid and Amanda approached me. I flinched, but they were chummier than ever, linking arms with me and laughing.

'Got your shoes back then? Don't look so down in the dumps, like a mole, we were only joking!'

'Yeah, can't you take a joke? Cheer up, Moley.'

So I stayed with them timidly, trying to decipher the foreign language of their behaviour. Maybe I had spent too much time away from them and had forgotten how to play. They were alternately cold and pally between lessons – I went with them for lunch, but was never sure if I would be ignored or included. Three weeks passed before I finally chose aloneness over their so-called friendship. One morning before assembly they turned on me again, suddenly and for no apparent reason. I was thrown backwards onto the floor and dragged by my heels around the classroom several times, so my hair and clothes gathered the dirt from people's feet, and my own feet were so sore I could not stand for some time.

That I held to my vegetarian beliefs is testimony to their authenticity. Although I avoided Squid and Amanda as best I could from then on, they followed me, making rude remarks about my skinniness, or scraping the backs of my shoes with the toe of a boot so I would trip and my heels would bleed. Once they cornered me in the cloakrooms, stalling and bluffing for a while, until Squid had an idea.

'Smack her, I bet she won't do anything.'

Amanda slapped me hard across the face with her open palm. It stung. I was dizzy with a poisonous mixture of anger and misery, but Squid knew me well by then: I would not do anything. There was simply no chapter about such behaviour in my inner manual of life, so I did not know what to do. It was one of my most frightening realisations to date: if I could not defend myself at twelve, how would I survive the adult world? Why was cruelty to people more acceptable than cruelty to animals anyway? How could someone be against war and apparently against peace at the same time? Why was Squid thought to be a good name, and Mole was an insult? What was a proper reaction? Doing nothing seemed wrong, but so did hitting someone, even if they hit first. Why did I have to be in a world where such questions even arose? School did not provide answers to those sorts of questions; things made less and less sense the longer I stayed there.

That term two people in our class had birthday parties at their respective homes: one boy and one girl. I was the only person in the whole class of thirty who was not invited to either. Even Gilbert was invited by the boy, although he never went to parties. Gilbert was a deliberate nerd; he never had any friends and everyone made fun of him, but he did not seem to mind. He wore big glasses and *Brylcreem*, and went train spotting at weekends. He was a self-made authority on politics and martial arts, neither of which he actually practised, but that did not stop him lecturing people on both until they were practically keeling over with boredom. In the social structure, nerds at least had their own zone of existence. There was no zone for people like me. Maybe there were not actually people like me; I did not know what I was, but I was apparently something entirely outside society.

The dents in my confidence highlighted me as an easy target. A girl called Melanie, in the year above, singled me out for special attention. She did not know Squid or Amanda, she did not live in my village, I had never even noticed her before, but suddenly she was everywhere. Her eyes naturally bulged outwards like a toad's, and there seemed to be nobody living behind them. Her hair stood out at strange angles, dyed in mongrel patches of maroon, russet and gingery-blonde. She had a sallow complexion and her shoulders rounded inwards, giving a curve to her back like a crouching vulture even when she was standing. I first met her when she ripped my bus pass out of my hand one day as I waited to leave, and tossed it into the restive crowds. It was a striking introduction. Naturally I did nothing, except to scrabble on the ground for the little blue card that would let me go home. From then on, whenever I saw her, I felt like I was sinking.

I had found a secret set of lavatories where not many people bothered to go. I could generally be sure of not being spat on there at lunchtimes if I was quick, but Melanie stole even that pathetic luxury from me. She was skulking in the entrance one day with someone from her unwholesome gang, and would not let me pass without giving her money. When I declined the offer, she slid her hand inside her jacket and pulled out a flick knife, pressing it open and jabbing it madly towards my face in a single movement. I ran for my life, or so I thought. She did not chase me; it was apparently enough of a victory just to see me running. Her cackles echoed up through the vestibule.

* * *

Granddad was suddenly dying of cancer. Although I was not allowed to see him, the descriptions of his pain and rapidly wasting body were enough for me to imagine the rest. He passed away relatively quickly: a mixed blessing. I was worried not so much by the death itself, but by the devastation it left behind. At the time to me aloneness was worse than any fate. That was all my dear Nanny had left: aloneness and a wardrobe half full of his clothes. She could not even stand at the funeral service; her daughters had to prop and heave her away when the time came to leave. I cried much more for her than for Granddad, and dreaded the day I would be in her shoes. Did not every woman face the same destiny?

God was almost forgotten by then, perhaps when I needed Him most. Swamped by my daily struggle, beauty and joy were neither valuable nor even noticeable; things were only measured by their contributions to survival or escape. I was glad to avoid school over summer, but knew it was just a temporary release. Fourteen, fifteen and adulthood were my only prospects, and they would surely prove yet more complicated. The single benefit to an advance in age seemed to be an increase in freedom, but the challenges far outweighed that gain. My innate fear kept pace with me as I grew, and seemed to be hardening into something more permanent. The notions of goodness and innocence were gone, apparently forever.

My room had been refurbished with a new carpet, and even had its own black and white television. I was allowed to watch quietly until any time of night, as long as I got up at a decent hour in the morning. Although there were not as many programmes on in those days, I always found something to help me evade the constant worries until sleep embraced me. Drowsing late one night, I found a documentary about a hypnotist who regressed people back to the time before they were born. A current of alertness bolted through me as different people claimed to unveil their previous lives. It was the first time I had heard the word 'reincarnation.' The tales of the participants were not necessarily convincing, but the concept of rebirth was more a remembering than a revelation. Like the tiny flame of a match, it gave me vague yet tangible bearings on my own existence. Time had gained a new dimension. My perpetual fear had gained a possible explanation, although I could not name its source. It did not seem anchored to anything real, and yet it was more familiar to me than all other emotions combined. In the light of many lives, I could assume it had survived with me from another time: perhaps a time when my terror was justified. Although it was some comfort, it was not a solution. Part of me wanted to know the truth about my past, but the fear itself was enough to carry, without having to drag the weight of memories with me as well.

I wandered into another programme one night, about Western devotees of Sri Krishna. They spoke openly about spirituality, and gave demonstrations of chanting, alone or in groups. Some of the women wore Indian saris, which I thought strange, but genuine joy and goodness glowed on all their faces. That powerful natural happiness seemed to set them apart from other people even more obviously than their choice of clothing; they certainly looked a world apart from the grim image in my own mirror. The paintings of Sri Krishna on the screen, although only monochrome, were more beautiful than any pictures I had ever seen. They looked fondly familiar, perhaps just by dint of their divinity. The male devotees shaved their heads, and left a little bunch behind, by which Sri Krishna could pull them up to Heaven at any time. That idea besotted me. For some reason the women wore their hair long, but undeterred by my gender, I went to the bathroom and pulled my fringe back from my face, trying to picture myself as bald with a long tuft at the back. I almost dared myself to shave it right then, and the thrill of that intensity took me outside the petty details of my life. I heard canned laughter coming from the television downstairs though, and imagined the reality of my mother's face when she saw me. Then I pictured Melanie coming at me with a flick knife and Sri Krishna pulling me up at the final second, her devilish grin then deflating into bewilderment. The canned laughter came again to snap me out of my fantasy. In the end I got some nail scissors and just cut the sides down to a thumb's width, like a tame, flat Mohican. My mother noticed, but she did not say anything.

When I returned to school in autumn, Squid had disappeared. I heard Amanda telling someone she had moved Down South. From then on Amanda hung around with two girls from the year below and mercifully ignored me, so I almost stopped noticing her altogether. An equally happy discovery was the new Head of Art. He went through the world with a melancholy bundled around all of his movements and speech. I liked that; I had not seen any of my own feelings reflected in a teacher before. He was a teenager in a man's body, complete with a slouch and a mumble. Nobody talked back to him; he hinted at a temper that might not have had boundaries if it got started. Although the kindling was stacked up ready for a flame, never so much as a spark came near him. His opinions and theories had a flourish of rebellion, yet with a depth beyond the ken of an average thirteen-year-old.

I had always drawn at home, so art classes were like break times without the bullying. One could learn life skills in art, not just the mechanics of drawing. Erasers were forbidden: they were apparently for cowards and cheats, and I did not fancy either label. The theory was that we must not be afraid of making a mistake, meanwhile giving each stroke our full attention in order to make it as perfect as possible. It seemed to me a good philosophy for anything. Copying another's style was also forbidden: that rule certainly went against the general teenage grain. Art was the only lesson in which self-expression was encouraged. In all my other subjects – history, geography, liter-ature, languages, mathematics, biology and even religious education – there was only ever one right answer to which everyone must adhere. In art the only correct response was to view the truth through one's own unique eyes and to render it in lines. Such freedom had to be bought with courage. Although I thought I lacked that quality in a combative sense, I realised for the first time that it had coursed through my every cell and sentiment since the day I was born.

'Courage is not the absence of fear,' announced the teacher in a rare glimmer of passion, 'but perseverance in the face of fear.'

Those words were as if crafted only for me. The news turned my world inside out. Maybe I would never be without fear, but I knew I could persevere in spite of it: I had always done so.

Perhaps it was my artistic confidence that brought me a new friend, or maybe it was my narrowed hairstyle; strangely we had both in common. She was called Andrea, which I gradually turned into Candy over the following months. She had an arrow-shaped nose with long nostrils that she used to express alarm or disapproval. Her skin was freckled and ruddy, matching her sunny and frivolous nature. She called me Petal.

School was infinitely more bearable with a real friend, with an ever-increasingly threatening hairstyle, and very particular interpretations of uniform guidelines. Candy's natural effervescence made her popular with everyone – girls and boys alike – so we were both invited to parties without a second thought. I was readily accepted just by being her favourite, even by those who previously pretended I did not exist.

Candy and I were similarly matched in our subjects, except she had a significant head start in Religious Education. Having been brought up a Catholic, Sunday school and Bible studies were workaday for her, even though she never confessed to any faith of her own. Religious Education was compulsory at school. The teacher was known as Patsy. Calling a teacher by the first name was forbidden, especially to the face; such humiliation was worse than even the rudest nickname, and was reserved only for Patsy. She took it as her mission to bring God to the most depraved and uncontrollable, and had already carried that cross for many years, but her sacrifice did not seem to be bearing any obvious fruit. Patsy's skin was almost translucent, with her bones and veins protruding from under it. She spoke in a nasal whine and wore thick glasses like a pair of mounted bottle ends. All of her lessons seemed a waste of everybody's time, as did the homework, which usually comprised illustrating scenes from the Bible that she had told in class. Her one request was that we never try to depict Satan, even if he was mentioned. I would usually add a red cloven hoof to the corner of my drawings, or sometimes the charred prongs of a fork, whether he was mentioned or not. It was not true rebellion, but just another bizarre form of self-preservation, like a choice of hairstyle or seat on the bus. God was Himself a laughing stock, so I buried all my earlier notions of Him and learned never to sing in assembly. I decided popularity was more tangible and reachable than He was, and I was quite sure I could live without Him anyway.

I longed to be a fifth-year, when there would be nobody pressing down on me anymore at school, apart from the perennial scourge of teachers, and the sixth-formers, who seemed only interested in study. My only real threat was still Melanie, and thankfully she was soon in her final year. On the last day of summer term one of her clan was waiting for me in the bus park, to inform me that Melanie was going to 'kick my head in' at lunch time. It was almost a compliment that I was to be her last feature fight before she went out into the world, but the reality would of course be grisly. I knew I could not defend myself, and would thus be beaten by all of them at once, possibly with weapons. I blanched, and my legs grew numb, but I somehow found my way to the safety of my first lesson. Candy was already rushing towards me as I opened the door.

'I know, I just heard. I'm not going to do it.'

'She's not going to let you off, she can't be expelled now, or even suspended!'

'This can't be happening.' All the air and strength poured out of me, and I stared into nothing.

My classes were a blur. It should have been a happy day, with weeks of lazing around ahead of me, and a list of summer barbecue invitations. The sweat prickled in the neck of my shirt and my throat felt dry and itchy. The bell for lunch was like my own death knell.

'I'm going to Kenzie,' I burst out, 'and you're coming with me.'

'Kenzie? No chance, I'm not going up there!'

'Hide your nail varnish, you're coming with me. If they can't find me, you might be next.'

Kenzie – short for a convoluted, double-barrelled surname – was the head of the upper school. It was lunacy to even cross his path voluntarily, but the alternative was unthinkable. I had been sent to him only twice previously to confess misdemeanours: once it was my fault, once it was not, but the experience was equally unpleasant. Even the corridor housing his office seemed to have an invisible repellent force around it, like a magnet in reverse. There were four or five ruffians queuing outside with their shirts hanging out, trying to seem carefree, but with an obvious air of impending doom. We joined the end of the line, Candy shifting from one foot to the other with her sleeves pulled over her hands; I slumped against the wall in despair. Telling on people – 'grassing them up' – was not considered wise. It happened only rarely, even under pressure: the social conse- quence of grassing was far worse than any sentence given by a teacher for the original crime, so it was simply uneconomical. Had it not been Melanie's last day, the plan would probably have backfired.

'What are you two doing here?' snapped Kenzie, pivoting through the doorway on his shiny brogues.

I explained and Candy interjected. He nearly dismissed us, but thought better of it at the last minute, marching us into a box room across the hall that he used for detention. On a brilliant July day, especially the eve of the holidays, being shut indoors would normally have been a punishment; that day it was our salvation. Our window overlooked the main courtyard, so we had a bird's-eye view of anyone walking round. After a few terrible minutes Melanie appeared, with four motley figures trailing behind. Her shirt was covered in signatures and messages, as was the custom for anyone leaving school forever. She leaned forward, stalking through the crowds like a hungry dog. Candy whooped with laughter, and clapped her hands. I just stared. Despite the midday heat, my every pore became a goose bump. Although there was some comfort in knowing Melanie's whereabouts, my nerves were so frayed I half expected a surprise attack, even in the relative safety of Kenzie's detention room. It was the longest hour of my life to date. The five appeared again and again – visibly hotter and angrier each time – until eventually the bell rang for the afternoon. I flattened onto a desk, limp with relief.

The only time I saw Melanie again she would have been seventeen, and was already pushing a baby pram along the high street. I almost did not recognise her, as her hair was thin and flat. Her glance passed straight through me, as if looking out from some parallel ghostly realm. Her eyes shifted fast like those of a hunted animal, all signs of hope replaced by a grey pall of bewilderment. Despite the torment she had caused me, I felt only pity for her then. Part of me thought I should be laughing, but I could only wince at her obvious misfortune. She looked more frightened and alone than even I had ever felt.

* * *

Socially the fifth year was a breeze, but it brought the harsh decisions of my future. The choice ahead was a luxury, but there was nobody to ask what to do anymore, and the freedom was suddenly unnerving. I was only certain of two ambitions: to leave school and to leave home forever. In the end I was destined for

Harrogate School of Art, alone. It was daunting, but it seemed like the only way to retain my sense of self, even if I lost the crutch of Candy's company.

My last party with her was the day I turned sixteen. The morning sky was a soft papery blue as the sun called out its jubilance. I had no sense of where my own coat of skin ended and the air around it began. Like some derelict motorcade, three beaten-up cars arrived to collect me, three similar tracks competing on their stereos through open windows. The lower part of the house buzzed briefly with assorted teenagers – some from our year in school, the rest Candy's older brother and his friends. The day and evening dissolved from then in spontaneous revelry.

'This is your day, Petal.'

Candy tapped her half of snakebite-and-black against mine. It was our signature drink for celebrations: cider and lager mingled together in a cheap but combustive cocktail, the blackcurrant syrup helping to make it feasible for the tongue. After a few shouts and cheers, we dropped our bare feet over the river Ouse. Nobody said much then, as nothing needed saying; the sparkle on the green water and our languid thoughts were enough. I felt I could never be cold, unhappy or unpopular again; that it would always be my day.

It was the summer for which my mother had always prepared me: the dawn of my independence. Having leapt straight from her own parental home into marriage, it was a freedom she herself had never known, much less at such a malleable age. I would receive a government grant of thirty-seven pounds a week for all my expenses, and I was determined it would be enough. Wherever I was heading, whatever I needed to get me there, I resolved to make do and get on with it.

4

Fame and Fortune

What is success?
Money-power.
What is success?
Fame-tower.

What is progress?
Oneness-height.
What is progress?
Perfection-delight. [4]
—Sri Chinmoy

Harrogate's steep terrain made it feel bleaker than anywhere in the colder months. I took a fusty bedsit off Cheltenham Parade for thirty-two pounds a week, leaving me five pounds for everything else. Reaching home from town meant passing a pizzeria called *Pinocchios*, flanking a corner with its wide plate windows. Pizza was by far my favourite food, but even the frozen sort was already out of my league. As the evenings drew in, passing that corner became a specific torture to me, but I could not resist looking in every time. The tables butted right up against the windows, and were set with candles in puckered red globes. I could almost have reached a slice from somebody's dish were it not for the glass between us. The smiles and laughter from inside gave an almost physical bolt of longing, as did the fragrances of fresh dough, roasting onions and melting cheese that wandered through the entrance. Instead I ate a lot of raw carrots, and potatoes cooked in many creative styles. There was a bakery on the way to college that sold fresh ring doughnuts painted with a thin crust of icing – they were only twelve pence each, so that was usually breakfast. The college offered subsidised meals, so I would have a portion of hot chips at lunchtime, as did most of my colleagues.

Wearing my own choice of clothes every day left me far more comfortable than ever before: socially and physically. Finally I had found a place where being myself was not only tolerable, but highly encouraged. The tutors spoke to us like intelligent adults instead of naughty juveniles; my peers were accordingly open and civil. However different we were from one another, there was a pervading sense of acceptance: a stark departure from the oppression and violence I had grown used to in school. There was nobody to tell me I was wrong or to remind me I was shy, so I dared imagine a life without either label. I was not so much reinvented as revealed: layers of confusion and inadequacy falling away like the casing of a seed as it shoots up to the sun.

In the first morning break I made three friends without trying, and we stuck together in the days that followed. Carla was a budding sculptress from Malta. She was short and curvy, her darkly gorgeous features undisguised beneath a blunt boyish haircut. She talked as much as the rest of us combined, and was thus probably what cemented us together in the first place. Pale and freckly with short russet hair, Lorna was already a year older than we were. She knew all the olden ways to dye things with rural plants. She could shear sheep by herself and build dry-stone walls, which impressed us all, but she neither needed nor warmed to anybody's praise. James was primarily a guitarist, but he had already grown weary of studying music. The only genre he could reasonably pursue in education was Classical, which he dreaded might only lead him to a stool in a restaurant, playing florid Flamenco to old ladies. James was the kind of person who could have done anything he chose, so he ended up doing nothing much at all. He was tall, angular and beautiful, with black hair in a ponytail. He smoked fat French cigarettes instead of the more common skinny roll-ups. He spoke softly and had a pensive air about him: in a poetic rather than a tragic way. Within a week Carla was 'in love' with James, and James was 'in love' with Lorna, whom he knew already had a long-term boyfriend. It was the sort of open-ended triangle of infatuation only artists could thrive on. Like a walking teenage diary, I was the listening ear to all their daily heartbreaks.

Most of our early days, and many of our later ones, were absorbed in charcoal drawing. I do not remember using anything as refined as pencil until my second year, and we were not allowed paint or coloured chalks until we had proven ourselves worthy of them. While it is true that a bad craftsman blames his tools, the supplies provided by the college were generally not enough to cover the work required of us. Charcoal was doled out in our rations, but however carefully we tended it, would often break or dissolve in the hand, drop to the ground and be crushed under foot, or fall out of its box in a bag, sullying sketch books, library books, and anything else that happened to be there. Although the art suppliers in town offered us a generous discount, a lot of my remaining grant still ended up in their pockets.

My funds had run out well before the end of the first term, and there was only a single pound left in my pocket. I paced the black streets, slick with drizzle, long into the evening, watching the fruit on the market stalls being packed into crates, the shop signs turning to CLOSED, the traffic thickening and diluting again as workers rushed home to their families and hot dinners. That pound was like a weight of responsibility that I was simply not strong enough to carry, but it was mine to bear. Like Tolkien's Frodo, I seemed to hold the most important thing in the world, but it was too complex and powerful for one so guileless as me. I crumpled on a bench beneath the cenotaph, feeling like a lost child. Nobody was looking for me though, or even waiting for me. I brooded there more sincerely than I ever had before, which did not help at all. Music then broke into my silent turmoil, making a haven of hope in my heart, like the eye in a storm. Someone was playing guitar on a street corner, and a man's voice was singing. It was only a tawdry love song, but he shaped it with feeling. I did not look at him, afraid of being disillusioned by his face, but dropped the pound in his guitar case as I passed, and carried on home. Although nothing was solved and nothing was changed, I was as a kite whose strings had been severed. I no longer had any weight at all and floated into a waking dream of contentment.

Carla had moved back to Malta by then, and James had fallen 'out of love' with Lorna. Lorna's boyfriend had moved to Harrogate and they had a little cottage together, so she did not spend much time with us anymore, at least not outside of college. James's 'love' was not so ardent as to prompt a duel over her anyway; he admitted it was mostly her unreachable nature that had made him want to reach her in the first place, and her coldness ultimately bored him.

On the last day of term, the college arranged a coach trip to London for all of us, so we could visit exhibitions. The classrooms were a frenzy of anticipation, but there was one thing bothering James: he lived with his family, twelve miles away in Ripon. The coaches would come back to Harrogate after midnight, so there would be no way home. I said without a blink he would be welcome to stay. It was common for people to end up 'dossing' on one another's floors; it meant nothing at all. James and I spent the whole day in London together. He knew the city well, and we both loved it equally. Our conversations stretched across the bus trip home and on into the dawn, sitting at my bedsit window.

The next evening I found myself on the inside of *Pinocchio's* at James's invitation. Just being the other side of that restaurant window at last was enough joy for me in itself, but I had no idea how the winds of my fortune were changing.

'Why do you live in that stodgy old room?'

'It's all I can afford.'

'But you can't afford it.'

'No, I know.' I chuckled at my blown defences, trying not to tear off unladylike chunks of hot pizza as my instincts were suggesting.

'Come and live at my parents' place, they won't mind.'

'Seriously? Wouldn't you need to ask them first?'

'Not really, but I can if you want. Come and meet them tomorrow, you'll see.'

Richard was an architect who had taken early retirement the previous summer. He and his wife Rosemary had moved to Yorkshire from Suffolk, to start a family bookshop. The handsome market city of Ripon, with its medieval cathedral and gentle green surrounds, seemed an ideal situation. James had a suite that took up the entire attic: two vast rooms with gabled windows, and a bathroom bigger than my whole bedsit. Apparently I would not be in the way – a whole additional family could probably live up there quite comfortably without ever being seen.

James had decided not to go back to college in the second term. He did not really need to earn his keep, but he amused himself at the bookshop while deciding what to do next. Even when I was physically away from him at college, I recorded in my mind everything that happened in the course of a day, so I could run to tell him afterwards. Likewise I was greedy for his every detail. We moulded into a flawless symbiosis, increasingly wonderstruck that two human beings could be so familiar, and yet had survived the world for sixteen years without knowing of the other's existence. We laughed at the same things, chose the same flavours, spoke each other's thoughts, and marvelled at the same works of art or nature. I was no longer just me, but one half of 'us' – an entity whose two equal slices fitted together with no discernible join. It was a perfect life in a perfect world, and my eyes were more open than ever before.

I carried a sketchbook with me all day, in which to record shapes and negative spaces, perspectives, textures and hues as best I could. There was beauty in everything: too much beauty to even observe, let alone to replicate. My lessons absorbed me totally, and I strove with all my heart to improve. I looked from closer and from further away; I looked from every angle, from inside and out. My clothes and shoes were haphazardly decorated with oil paints in every colour. Any books I carried with me, or anything made of paper, grew dabs of colour, each in a circle of yellow oil. My hands always smelled of linseed and turpentine.

Some days I did not have important lectures, so to save the bus fare I stayed in Ripon and helped in the shop. It was on top of a pretty arcade in the city centre: modest in size, but stocked to the ceiling with books, solely on art and spirituality. Art was all I wanted at the time, so I gazed at the glossy prints or peeped inside the biographies while dusting them. James would take me to one of the local cafés afterwards; we always found money for tea and cakes, as well as something small to celebrate. I usually cooked dinner for the family in the evenings. James was vegetarian anyway, and the others did not seem to mind. In summer we would sit in the front garden, or in the first floor drawing room with the French doors open to the trees, sipping chilled rosé wine and listening to Richard's old jazz records. James and I would sometimes go for walks in the woods later, or along the river. The sun edged everything in pure gold. Everything. It did not exclude ugly or dirty things, like dustbin lids, grimy vans or abandoned shopping trolleys. All things were blessed and beautiful. Even the tiny midges playing over the water were anointed in just the same way. When we returned home, the house seemed more still and quiet than before, despite its usual bustle. Nature had a way of explaining life to me; it coaxed me to believe in magic and miracles again. James always spent any new inspiration on his guitar upstairs, and we often created strange songs together: I wrote oblique poems from my dreams and sang them to his curious melodies. When night came in earnest, we listened to our own records, or watched fifties B-movies, smoking fat French cigarettes in the dark.

At seventeen, my fear had a sudden growth spurt. As my heart had blossomed in the sunlight of love, it was necessarily open to all other weather too. It seemed an increasing artistic awareness meant an acute sensitivity to the world's savagery as well as its refinement. Everything was real and raw. I dreaded my future, just as I had done at school, but suddenly much more vividly. My emotions had become deeply invested in another human being – one who had never once let me down, but the potential power he held over me became unbearable. Instead of drawing back, I clung to James ever more closely. Often I missed college because I simply could not face any other than his company, and I was afraid to be in any room alone.

Within weeks, I spiralled into a complete emotional breakdown. I did not want life at all anymore, and fantasised about its ending. I cried for hours at a time, until I could barely open my eyes. Sometimes my wrenching sobs could even be heard on the floors below, and James or his mother would come to me. They trembled just at the sight of my face and body, twisted with inexpressible despair. My nightmares and even waking dreams became too horrible to repeat. I was plummeting head first into an ocean of darkness. Although he did the best he could, James was also only seventeen and ill-equipped for such a burden, so my condition started to tell on his health. It was Rosemary who showed me a glimmer of light, like a match flame, guiding me back to the shore in inches.

'God is the only One to help you. Whatever you need, whatever we cannot give you, He already has, you only have to ask Him. Just go to Him, you don't even need words, He already understands.'

'I think He's forgotten me.'

'I think you've forgotten Him,' she said, after a polite pause.

Luckily I knew for certain she was right, but He still seemed so far away.

'How will I know where He is?'

'Listen for Him through meditation.'

'I don't know how.'

'Lao-Tsu said, "A journey of a thousand miles begins with a single step." Just take one step today, the rest will follow.'

She promised to return within moments; it could have been hours for all I knew. I slumped down, so exhausted and relieved even at that brief revelation, I could have slept for days. A slender book was pressed into my hand: *Creative Visualization* by Shakti Gawain. Rosemary began to read from another book: *The Relaxation Response* by Herbert Benson. I was already sleeping again before the end of the first page.

Rosemary and her trove of spiritual books became my lifeline. I spent every penny I could find on more, and she gave me many more than I paid for. I devoured the new writings on the way to college, even when rain dashed sideways under my umbrella. Every evening, before doing anything else, I would practise hatha yoga for one side of a favourite cassette, and lie down for the other to try some of the meditation exercises I had read about. I wondered why I had not been taught anything so useful at school. Instead I had learned smocking stitch and the French for 'fishing rod', the workings of an earthworm's digestive system and ways to beat a coffee spoon out of copper. Such random knowledge was supposed to have equipped me for the world.

Ultimately I attained a merit in my diploma, but failed to earn a place for a degree. I took a summer job at a bakery, sometimes making cream cakes from five in the morning, then waitressing until five in the afternoon at the adjoining café. I was so flattened by the end of a day I spoke in monotone, and my feet made me believe my shoes had shrunk a full size. Still I gathered all my stubbornness to do it again the next day, often through stifled sobs of exhaustion. Although academically and artistically I had always been above average, I was apparently not born with any of the skills required of a waitress. I invariably forgot orders or brought things to the wrong tables; I dropped things, spilled things and generally got in the way. My mental arithmetic never rose above remedial level, so I often charged the wrong amount, or gave the incorrect change. I was fired from the café within three weeks, and was not invited back to bake as a result.

James's only dream by then was to have his own band, and to become a famous guitarist. I was necessarily woven into his ideals. He had befriended someone in Harrogate with a recording studio inside his house. We could put some of our songs onto a demo tape there, with which to seek out new opportunities. The idea thrilled me to the core; what teenage girl would not want to be lead singer in a famous band? We spent every remaining evening and weekend of summer at the studio, but often ended up smoking such quantities of weed that nothing much was achieved. Although in terms of productivity a lot of time was wasted, the studio opened a new world to me. My creative passion translated perfectly to music; the heightened awareness I had gained from art and meditation gave me freedom to explore the landscapes and playgrounds of sound. One of many downsides to smoking weed is that it makes everything seem more interesting than it really is. The tapes that had almost made us weep at their beauty the night before certainly lost their lustre by daybreak. I did learn new confidence though, and that was more valuable to me than anything I could have transferred to cassette anyway. Although a lot can be done to enhance the voice once it has been recorded, the microphone does not forgive fear. I worked hard to overcome my shyness in singing, which I hoped would translate to everyday life. That seemed itself a priceless life skill.

James's parents had decided to sell the shop and move back to Suffolk. They had already bought a large country cottage, and James suggested we go with them. We would stay there while we found our feet, transferring then to the relative metropolis of Ipswich. James had heard of a government scheme that would give us a grant to set up a business as musicians, so we could start a band and make money from concerts. It sounded far-fetched, but I believed in magic after all, and his enthusiasm was infectious. I had no better plan of my own, and being apart from him never crossed my mind.

* * *

A girl searched for breath between the tang of nicotine and the sweet cloy of dry ice. Two teenage lungs could barely fuel her voice above a morass of electric guitar, but she sang out as if for her life. She twirled barefoot, while the bass drum galloped on behind. Her knee-length frock coat fanned out in a wide fringe, its heavy weight of sequins, beads and buttons glittering wildly in the spotlights. Under a spangled skullcap and a thatch of white-blonde hair, flashed two tempestuous green-blue eyes.

Behind that stage persona, I did not know who I was; I only chased the terror and exhilaration of performing, to come alive as some invented individual. We all lived for music then: James and I, a drummer and a bass guitarist. Off-stage and especially in studios, we fought endlessly about everything, as everything mattered passionately to each. On stage we melded into one form, an emergent work of art. We would not cheapen ourselves for money or easy fame; there were no love songs, no synthetic rhythms, no revealing clothing, and thus sometimes very little audience. The others grumbled about their costumes – I made them myself, even shaping each button from clay and decorating it with fabric or paint. As lead singer, and the only girl, I won more than my share of arguments. We practised in the disused barn of a poultry farm. It was cold and dirty, full of old flies and chicken smells, but sound was like a magic carpet, taking us beyond all other senses, and far beyond our differences. At night, we dreamed in melody and rhyme.

We thought it was all very brave and bewitching at the time. Actually, apart from the music, it was squalid. James and I shared a room in a terraced house on Oxford Road, with people we did not know. Our scant income left little for rent and food, one cabbage and a loaf of bread often lasting two days. Mornings were always silent – everyone slept then, except us. We did not even dare to use the bathroom after noon. One look into the eyes of the drug dealer from the room next to ours was enough: they were only sockets of glassy emptiness, as if nobody lived inside them. All sense and reason, everything significantly conscious or responsive, had long departed his young body. In an eerie parallel, his domain was blacked out at the windows. A furtive glance inside revealed a dingy nest of bedclothes strewn among chicken bones, empty food packets and half-empty milk cartons. There had once been a payphone on the wall for everyone's use, but it was by then a charred and useless skeleton – he had melted the plastic casing so as to inhale the fumes. He ruled the corridor in which he lived, and the bathroom was at the end of it. When we suspected he was even partially awake, we bolted the door from the inside, or quietly left the house. We pitied him, but lived transparently to preserve ourselves, like ghosts haunting our own home.

Late in the day the arguments would start downstairs, and an electronic rhythm began thundering from the room next door. Often it was the same song repeated for hours at a time. The sound was like a boot kicking a bruise. One night when James was away, the bruise grew to unbearable proportions. The beat reached behind my earplugs and under the pillow, it throbbed in the very nails of the floor and rang in the springs of the mattress.

There seemed no escape except madness. Music had been my idol up to then, but suddenly it was my nemesis. I curled into a ball and whimpered like a wounded dog, entreating God for some release. As a man athirst is reduced to one single idea of water, I was a one-pointed longing for peace; I ached for it in my every nerve and breath. No price could have been too high. My desperation drove me to a new sincerity, and no doubt God took pity on me. I had practised meditation for almost a year, but only when the house was quiet. Could I, in my spiritual infancy, find power enough to rise above that hellish noise? I uncurled my body, unclenched my teeth and fists, and dared myself to let go. With little further effort on my part, meditation folded me in its soft wings and carried me far beyond all earthly pain. Although I could still hear the sound, and feel it coursing through the floorboards, it could not touch me. It became tiny, innocent, irrelevant, like the marching of an ant. For a few minutes I was wonder-struck, amazed not so much by meditation's power, but by my own capacity to hold it. The experience was short lived – only because I drifted from it without even noticing, far out into the oblivion of sleep. If God could find me in such a house, thought I the next morning, He really is everywhere.

James and I eventually moved to our own maisonette: part of a ramshackle house on London Road. We had a front door again, a clear boundary to the world outside, for which we were far more grateful having had to make do without. I was singing in the kitchen, arranging our things proudly on the shelves. As I slid the teapot from its newspaper wrapping, the lid shot to the floor and smashed into shards. Such a small thing would not have bothered me, especially not on that triumphant day, but the pot had been a gift from my last remaining grandparent. Nanny had never recovered from the loss of her husband. She was withering fast by then, riddled with cancer. The next day a letter was delivered express from my mother, to say she had passed away – it had happened just at the time the lid had fallen. My mother sounded wrung dry when I called, and as though the very muscles of her face were spent. I could hear she was peaceful though, even through the clunky public handset that always made people seem far away. For a month it had not really been Nanny in the hospital bed, but a faded puppet suspended only by threads of morphine, sleeping or speaking troubled nonsense. Although she was dearer to me than Granddad, her funeral was not so grim as his – she was not leaving half herself behind as he did, so there was not such a depth of sadness. I imagined her restored to her dainty youth as I had only seen in the wedding photographs: her cheeks too rosy with pink water-colour, her hair painted bright auburn in waves like silk ribbons. She clung childlike to her sweetheart's arm with hands like perfect porcelain. He wore a rare grin and a suit that looked like it was cut from cardboard; only the green in his buttonhole was coloured in. I brought home their cutlery set in its satin-lined cabinet, with the special forks and knives for fish that I knew I would not use. I polished them anyway, as Nanny would have done since the day she was married. I kept the teapot, even though it was useless without a lid.

James still represented human perfection to me, but I gradually realised something was missing. Although it was an odd, unfamiliar feeling, it did not frighten me. I knew neither where it had come from nor where it was leading me, but it grew such force my only choice was to follow it. I had not become disappointed or bored by him – that seemed impossible, as we were ideally suited – it was more a discovery that even he was not enough for me, and maybe no human being could be. I imagined fame would not be enough either, if it actually materialised, as we both believed. James had held the key to my every thought and plan, but for the first time I was at a loss to explain my heart to him. I became muffled and clumsy, as though walking through deep snow, the white falling faster in the air until I could neither see his face nor my own destination. I wished I could have been kinder instead of fumbling, but maybe there is no kind way to tell someone they do not belong anymore. Afraid to hear his tears falling, knowing they were my fault, I walked away: cowardly and courageous in equal measure.

I saw James only once more, a long time after. His music career had not taken off, at least not by then; he was working as a catwalk model. He had met another girl within a year or so, and seemed contented. She was young and sweet-faced. Her name was Jamie.

Nanny had left me ten thousand pounds. A sensible girl would have got a proper job and kept the savings, but freedom seemed far more precious than security at the time. I hoped the cosmopolitan metropolis of London would be like a crossroads with many signs, pointing to all the opportunities of the world. In fact surrounded by countless people who seemed to know what they were doing only left me more bewildered and alone. Up a hill behind my new home in Dulwich was a seat looking over the city. In the autumn evenings I would sink there into a comfortable melancholy, tracing the curve of the Thames and picking out the roof of St Paul's. Since starting to meditate, I was no longer afraid without reason; I had taken to testing my fear, turning on it and confronting it, to find it just dissolved like a creature of smoke. It was then that I stopped practising meditation: ironically, without the devastating weight of fear, stilling the mind every day seemed too laborious.

Curious to be on the other side of a canvas for a change, I sat part-time for a painter in Camden, but the stillness left too much time for brooding. Even London was not sufficient distraction from the half I had left behind; every day brought more occasions that would have charmed him, and my reflex to tell him did not wear away. Over months I scoured the city for ideas and clues of how to fill the space I had created. Still none came. What could I do with so much room inside? Who could possibly be enough to fill it? It seemed too large a lodging for just another person, or even a family.

At last I called my mother and asked to come back to York again so I could work things out. I decided to get a proper job, any job, just to root my feet in the ground. Sponging off the government and gnawing down my inheritance had eroded my self-esteem; I just wanted to be busy and to feel useful. There was a new outdoor-wear shop opening in Stonegate, so I started there as a sales assistant. It provided daily structure and a sense of achievement. Its customers – mainly zealots and adventurers – made for lively company. I loved the simple jobs like dusting shelves or tidying trouser legs: jobs that had a clear beginning and end, an obvious purpose and result. Compared to writing a song, or making five pounds last a week, or deciding what to do with my life, it was refreshingly straightforward. Sometimes after lunch I would walk to the Minster and sit in the nave. I was not meditating, or even praying really, but the grandeur silenced and intimidated me in a reassuring way. I liked to be reminded that I was small in the scheme of things: my problems were also small in that case. Looking at the sky, especially at night, usually had the same effect.

My mother had recently taken up running. I absolutely hated running, and had not even considered trying it since my repeated cross-country humiliations at school, but somehow she cajoled me into joining her for two miles every morning at seven o'clock. In winter it was dark, so we had to plod around the village, sometimes returning with our hair and eyebrows blown back in big white quiffs from the freezing fog. It did not please me, but I had to admit there was no better way to start the day. I gasped for my life in the first few weeks, but over months grew strong enough to keep pace with her. In spring and summer we used a country lane. The birds were already trying out their tunes when we joined them, the hedgerows already busy with life and green fragrances. I noticed the little things more while running. Maybe they helped take my mind off the gargantuan struggle of placing one foot in front of the other, but it seemed more than that – running heightened my awareness in a compelling way, reminding me that I was actually alive and not just a character in someone else's dream. Although I still was not meditating, running brought me a similar sense of calm – usually only when it was over, but sometimes before that.

I earned my keep at home by cleaning the house every week on my morning off. In the afternoon I often visited Candy, who was expecting her first child. She had left education at the same time as I had, but was married straight afterwards at eighteen, and could not have been happier with her choice. The couple lived on the edge of a mining town, in a damp terraced house that opened straight onto a road. She and I had imagined we would always be friends, but I realised then how different we were if such a life was enough for her. I always imagined I would have children too, as that was what people did. I was always sure that whatever I failed at, I would at least achieve motherhood, as it required no qualifications or prior experience. Seeing Candy swelling and staggering more each week, and eking out her housekeeping on the cheapest essentials, I began to wonder.

When the baby was born, I knew I would have neither the patience nor the stomach for childrearing. Candy named her Emily. She was a tiny miracle, fresh from Heaven: blonde-haired with perfect little rose-petal cheeks. I was glad for all of them, and touched by the naming, but apart from that, completely and silently baffled. Just the open discussions of human functions, the ever-growing collection of plastic accoutrements, the persistent smells of milk and talcum powder, were enough to leave me certain I was not of motherly stock. The things most people coo about just made me want to run away.

5

The Deep and the Degree

The outer education
Is
A fleeting knowledge.

The inner education
Is
A lasting experience. [5]
—Sri Chinmoy

An acquaintance from London called one day: a British ex-pat called Martin, living in Alabama. His girlfriend had left him just after he had bought a scuba diving holiday in Mexico, including lessons for her. He was not calling for consolation; there was already a new girlfriend by then, only she did not want to leave her children behind, and he did not want to take them. Everyone he thought of had a partner or was too busy, and he was determined not to let it go. Then he remembered me, whom he barely knew, but thought would be an interesting and trouble-free companion.

Martin had been an alcoholic since he was twelve. He finally kicked his thirty-five year addiction only two years before I met him. It was as if his childhood senses had been paused for all that time, and were suddenly released to the world in a big happy effusion. He was spontaneous, gregarious, yet with a dauntless innocence that I had never seen in anyone over about fourteen, let alone forty. I would pay my own way to America, and everything would be taken care of from there. There is no knowing what

Martin told his new girlfriend or his own three children – who were my age – but somehow he convinced them of the truth that we were innocent friends. In fact we were hardly even that.

The only obstacle was my fear of deep water. Those who ventured beyond the shallow end of a pool I crowned in my mind as heroes, and as veritable demigods those who would dive head first from a board. Those who would wade out far enough to lose their footing in the ocean, I labelled as reckless dolts who did not properly value the life they had been given. It was a highly rational fear as far as I was concerned: Candy had forced me to watch *Jaws* on a night of babysitting, so I knew what could happen at sea. Living inland, I had not faced that special terror for a long time, and it would not easily be varnished over on a diving holiday.

I admitted all of it to Martin, but he would not take no for an answer. Tired of toting fears on my shoulders, I decided it was time to face the deep once and for all. It was a bizarre and unlikely situation, but it seemed to have come to me on a plate: like first prize in some women's magazine competition that one assumes nobody actually wins. In the end I viewed it gravely as a service, and half hoped more specific excuses would come to mind if the deep really ended up being too deep for me. When harboured and reinforced for nearly twenty years, even the most rational fear can reach irrational proportions, so I could not vouch for my own responses.

I completed my training and gained my diving license, graduating from the shallow end to the deep end of a pool somewhere in Alabama, then to the murkier regions of a former quarry. I would use up my air in half the time of my peers due to my anxiety, but would not be deterred by any amount of ridicule. Eventually, after considerable private tuition and personal determination, I set off for the Caribbean island of Cozumel.

Martin had to pull out of his first dive due to painful sinuses, and ironically spent the rest of his time on land: eating nachos, reading the paper, and making sorrowful calls to his girlfriend. I think we both wondered what we were doing there in the end, but we made the best of it in our own separate ways.

With all the outer paraphernalia and inner baggage, I had to be pushed off the boat on my first adventure in the open sea. I was enraptured though, from the first moment. The harsh sun, the growl and fumes of the boat engine, the nauseous movement of the waves, even the weight of the equipment, were all replaced by cool purity and gentleness beneath the ocean's skin. Fear turned to awe as I entered a world where I did not belong, yet which had ample room to house me. I was humbled to float in a medium of which my own human body was largely composed, but which alone would not sustain it for more than a few seconds.

Up to then such tranquillity was unknown to me, but it seemed a perfect natural state. My breathing became even slower than it was above the surface, and I used less air than others. There was no sound except that breath: the husky drawing in, and the chink of exhalation, releasing plumes of amorphous bubbles. Colours were completely new; their hue and luminosity changed constantly, with a freedom unknown to the flatter shades of land. Freedom of movement in all directions was also new, like a dream of flying, although my own mammalian efforts took me nowhere compared to the sleek agility of sea creatures. Stillness became my favourite practice, controlling the posture and breath to balance inches from the seabed. Movement without effort was the crowning joy, drifting with the tide over coral gardens, tiny fish hovering and darting, like bees over blooms.

The creatures seemed to look on us as bumbling enigmas. They showed neither irritation nor fear that we were with them, knowing any lazy flinch of theirs would outsmart us. Many seemed hospitable, even taking time from apparently busy schedules to play games. The beauty, power and harmony of that strange environment etched themselves on my mind: a flock of eagle rays emerging into view, their massive wings forming slow graceful arcs, suspended like angels in a saline cathedral; the ugly glance of grouper snatching chunks of raw fish from my pocket; the specific majesty of depths beyond a hundred feet. I imagined the form of a shark would have caused me to expire with fright a few weeks before, but in reality its beauty disarmed me, and I saw only the perfection and efficiency of movement. In the deep, to my surprise, I met God in myriad beguiling guises. Tears crept out of my mask and mingled with the greater brine.

Our Dive Master was called Miguel, and claimed to be of purebred Mayan ancestry. He was accordingly short in stature but immensely strong, fine-featured and aflame with vigour. He was kind and patient, highly attentive to the ways of nature, and with a roguish sense of humour. Miguel and I shared the boat on an early dive with a honeymooning couple, who expressed an interest in night diving. The thought of being encased in blackened sea made me cringe with horror, but Miguel's enthusiasm soon held us all equally in its sway. Partly out of curiosity, and partly to chase out that new fear, I agreed to join them.

The couple did not turn up, so just Miguel and I sallied out into the darkness. There was no boat; we were to tumble backwards from a pier into that black void, hands clasped like a joint promise, on the agonising count of three. At first I thought I would dissolve in my own fright. I realised after several moments I had not let go his hand, and was probably cutting off the blood to his fingers with the vice of my own. We sank directly downwards, and I found we were not even as far out as the first coral shelf. Familiar wrinkles of sand were caught in the beam of his torch. Standing there quietly a while, I finally raised my free hand in the shape of *okay*.

I knew our destination was a wrecked plane very near the shore. I also knew it was not a real wreck, but one staged for a film in the seventies. I would never have had the will or nerve to visit a watery grave, especially at night. Creatures and coral had sheltered there and grown around it for so many years it looked like a miniature subterranean city. Colours were different in the torch light than in the bluish rays of the sun, but their beauty was in no way diminished. New faces peeped out as we arrived, or came with boldness to inspect us.

I had never thought to understand the octopus; until I met one, it was not more than an ignorant mass of jelly and rubber to me. Drawn to the light, one waved and curled above the ocean floor, eyeing us with its tilted bulbous head, and shimmying closer. *There You are!* I thought. Miguel stretched out his hand and God-in-octopus-form wound a foot-long leg around him, fastening more and more suckers to the arms of his wetsuit. He prised it away gingerly before it could attach itself, and passed it to me. I felt only gentleness, intelligence and childlike curiosity. I dared even sense affection.

There were countless illumining social visits before we journeyed back to the beach. Rather than relief, I knew only disappointment at the heft of my own body on land again. We gathered our equipment in silhouette by the light of the shore, and I turned to thank the ocean. I thought I had imagined its reply, but tiptoeing closer it was clearly real: a fluorescent glow on the crest of every ripple. As my hand stroked along its surface, each point of contact glowed with natural yellow-green sparkles. Maybe Miguel was touched by my reverence, or maybe he made a habit of inviting foreign girls to dinner. Either way we spent every evening together until it was time for me to go home. We carried on our correspondence from far sides of the world, and I vowed to return to Cozumel at Christmas.

Miguel was having a little house built inland. He casually proposed marriage at New Year, and I casually accepted. I had already become a cliché, and I did not care who knew it. I was only twenty, but world-weary, disillusioned with the struggle of living, and absolutely ready for retirement. I fell in love more with the idea of a languid Caribbean life than with Miguel, and perhaps he fell in love more with the idea of an English wife than with me, whom he did not know well enough to love. It was the only time in my life I was possibly found attractive for my material wealth.

Miguel's family was so large it seemed he was related in some way to every island inhabitant. There were maybe ten siblings, each themselves with many children. His uncles had their own Mariachi band and played in the streets or restaurants. The family followed their own branch of Catholicism that incorporated other rituals, perhaps grown out of ancient Mayan traditions.

One sister lived in a single room with her family – they all slept in hammocks hooked into the ceiling. The children were bundles of beaming smiles, bare feet and glossy black hair. They held my hands, made new names for me and dressed my head with wildflowers. In a next-door hut was the church, for which another sister was the priest. Forty or fifty met there several times a week, crowding together on bare wooden benches. The children played on the sandy ground at the back, or clambered on any of the adults, so one could not tell who belonged to whom. I had no idea what was said through it all, but felt a powerful force of goodness such as I had never known anywhere. Although the heat was initially extreme, within moments I forgot my own physical comfort and tears traced through the dusty sweat on my face. It was neither sadness nor agitation – only a general sense of relief and gratitude, without any particular thought or reason.

The priest was all in white, seated in a tall chair edged in white satin and silk flowers. After the formal service, she went into a trance that made her shudder and utter indistinct sounds. People could then ask her for advice, displaying their personal troubles to the room without shame or shyness. Her responses overflowed with love and surety. Everything was simple, natural, happy and honest, but with a depth I could feel much more than understand. After the questions were finished, food and household items – brought by the congregation – would be blessed and distributed. Miguel always brought a bottle of water scented with Lily of the Valley, to douse his boat and thus keep it safe. Other people brought cleaning products to sanctify their houses as they did their daily chores.

Returning home was a wrench, especially in winter, and I was already homesick for Mexico when the plane heaved itself off the ground. I resolved to move back there as quickly as possible, dividing my things into those for storing, those for selling, those for giving away and those I could not live without.

Then, while looking for my final one-way flight, I drew back suddenly, as if I had put my hand on a stove. I knew in an instant I was denying my fate, stepping off the pitch instead of playing the game.

Telling Miguel was unthinkably hard. By phone and letter he pleaded with me to change my mind, repeatedly and tearfully for several weeks, but just as with James, I felt the decision had already been made on my behalf. It was not the time for marriage, and Miguel was not the person. It was certainly no time for retirement. I had shocked even myself with my careless attitude to immense decisions. I wondered how I had fallen into such a daze, and shuddered at how late I came to my senses. Nature had beguiled me, the people's warmth and the heat of the sun had allured me, but those were no grounds for marriage, and possibly not even emigration.

* * *

In an effort to cover my foolish tracks, I decided to settle in any place that housed no prior memories. I was still a sales assistant, but had been acting as deputy manager for almost a year. An official promotion meant moving to another city, so that seemed a good solution. There was already a vacancy in Bristol.

Everything was agreed in principle; I would only have to visit the branch and let the manager see me.

As I packed to leave, my mother asked me into her room, to give me something she had been saving for my twenty-first birthday. Although a little early, my departure day seemed like a good time. It was Nanny's engagement ring: a simple loop of white gold, clutching a single sizeable diamond. The jewel seemed to blaze with a light of its own, and mesmerised me as much with its outer perfection as with its emotive symbolism. The band had been expanded at some point and fitted perfectly on my middle finger, so it stayed there, like an anchor to an age of happiness.

It was a frozen day in February when I first saw Bristol. Everything, including the sky, had the life and colour drained from it, like an iced lollipop with the juice sucked out. The shop was in a fine location by the river, so my reaction to it made no sense. The whole site was like a magnet turned backwards: the same repellent force as I used to feel around the Headmaster's office at school. The door stuck, so I forced it in to the small cheerless interior, and it clamped shut again behind me. The only person inside was a tall man, tidying a shelf. As he turned to greet me, I felt a sudden weight of darkness, as if I had never been happy and would never be happy again. I could neither explain it to myself nor shake it off. I badly wanted to leave, but somehow knew this person was a part of my destiny, and that the route ahead was treacherous.

Tom, as I then knew him, was ostensibly average. He looked in his late twenties, and apart from his height was of medium build. A faintly Welsh accent, high cheekbones and a self-assured stance were the only features distinguishing him. His questions were perfunctory, without notable depth or suspicion, delivered in a friendly yet professional manner. It was settled in the span of moments: I would start within a fortnight, and be given a further fortnight's lodging in a local hotel, allowing me time to find a home.

My legs felt wooden and clumsy as I walked to the train station, my empty gaze lowered to the pavement, the inexplicable sadness growing thicker and heavier like a private storm in my head. Hunched on a seat by the platform, I stared into the sign saying *Bristol*. How could an unfamiliar name put a knot in my stomach? How had a stranger – an ordinary man – filled me with such uncommon dread? I was cold to my bones, and could not remember feeling any other way.

Tom booked me a room off Whiteladies Road: an artery linking the city to a large green area of parkland called the Downs. I was on the Clifton side, which he recommended as a place to live permanently. I soon found a long-term lease, sharing a garden flat on Pembroke Road with a policewoman and her nervous grey cat. There were already signs of spring nosing through the earth. I took a weekend to explore the Downs, as well as Clifton Village with its old-fashioned shops and enclaves of wealthy stone houses. Brunel's Suspension Bridge jutted out from the cliff itself – a spindled tightrope for cars to cross the estuary, spangled with fairy lights at night. I knew most of my salary would go on rent, but lodging in such pleasant surrounds absorbed at least some of my gloom.

The shop was not nearly as busy as the one in York. We had two part-time girls, but mostly it was just Tom and I. Ordering was done centrally, so apart from banking and stock checking, there was little to do on quiet days. We thus got to know each other very quickly, although the more I knew about Tom the more I realised I did not know, and perhaps would never want to know. He shared a house with two other lads in Southville: an area on the far side of the river, beyond a stark patch of dockland. At first I could not understand why he had recommended Clifton for me, yet chose to live somewhere half as expensive himself – especially on a manager's salary – but his priorities were only gym membership and copious intakes of alcohol. He cared nothing for comfort or aesthetics.

As a manager, Tom was straightforward: helpful to the customers, and exemplary to his staff and superiors. As a person, he was far more complicated. His character at once enticed and repulsed me. He was quick-witted but crude, and away from the customers swore more than anyone I had met. By the same token he was vegetarian, because he abhorred the suffering of animals. He would often stop on the pavement to save a worm or a snail, and march out to the riverside if he saw so much as a seagull harassing a pigeon. Sometimes he was almost unbearably vulnerable and childlike in his kindness, but it always came with strangeness.

'What on earth are you doing?' I asked one day when the rain was lashing into the windows, and not a single customer had come in. Tom was kneeling on the floor with a box from one of the deliveries flattened in front of him. He had already sketched out an oblong with two circles embedded in one side.

'I'm making you a bus so you don't get wet on the way home.'

He proceeded to spend the best part of half an hour decorating the 'bus' with different colours, then adding various passengers at the windows, each with some amusing and long-winded reason for travelling.

'Let's go out for dinner at the weekend,' he said as we were lifting the grills onto the door and adding the rain-soaked padlocks. I was not sure if he felt sorry for me because I was new to the city, or if it was some managerial team-building exercise, or if he was asking me on a date. I had the feeling he did not know either. By then the reason did not matter, I was curious enough to accept. He was not at all to my taste, but I was drawn to him nonetheless, in a way I could not understand. The same power that had repelled me and filled me with dread had reversed without me realising: he was reeling me in to the strange vortex of his world.

I certainly did not love him, but somehow became addicted to him, and thus adopted his own addictions. I joined the gym along the river, and trained hard there every day after work, growing accustomed to lycra leotards and the scent of other people's sweat; learning mental defences against the stares of men and the taunt of full-length mirrors. Sometimes in the mornings I would go back for another workout before the shop opened, challenging the fog of my hangover. Although the increase in fitness was good, it was easily cancelled out by alcohol. My attitudes to everything quickly became unbalanced – I was thrashing my body like a mule, the self-induced struggle serving only to dull the colours of my emotion and veil the shapes of my future.

Tom eventually confided that he had been physically abused as a child. The memory preyed on his every happiness; it twisted his view of the world and complicated anything more personal than working life. I knew he was fond of me, but choked by his own pain he drew me in to his life, only to throw me out again, only to draw me in. It was maddening, but I was spellbound beyond my own reasoning. I had become like a dog running to the random sounds of its owner's whistle.

After a few months, I could no longer afford Clifton. I also wanted to be nearer Tom, in case he thought he needed me for something at short notice. To avoid eating further into my remaining morsel of inheritance, I moved to a grungy, noisy house in Southville, sharing with four student girls. My dignity and self-esteem were dripping away down a seemingly bottomless drain, but I was determined not to let them run dry. I knew my addiction to Tom, and all that entailed, was at the root of it. Perhaps leaving him, and leaving Bristol, would put an end to it for good.

I began to wonder if my father had been right all along: maybe success and money were more important than I had realised. I decided unless I tried that route, I would never know. Working in a shop, especially in the throes of recession, I was not going to find out very easily. A higher education might have helped, but I seemed to have narrowed my chances of that when I chose art over academia. I hoped to study business, but there was only one university that would take people like me for anything other than artistic subjects. It was the only private university in the country, and while it had an open mind about accepting students, the fees were exorbitant. I called my mother and told her everything. I was not asking for a solution, and I knew she had no more spare money than I did – I only wanted to open my heart to her. She was much bolder about it all than I was though, and came to a conclusion I would not have dared consider: asking my father to foot the bill. To our combined delight, he agreed. I was saved from the downward spiral of emotional attachment and the corresponding financial ruin. Dizzy with gratitude, I promised to work hard, and longed to win my father's pride.

While I was sorry for Tom's pain, I was obviously powerless to ease it, and was only ruining myself by trying. I asked him very clearly never to contact me again, to which his response was stony and silent. I did not know what that meant, so I took it as a sign that he had no opinion. I walked away at last, as I had so wanted to do when I first saw him.

* * *

The fastest time one could attain a degree at my new university was two years. Anyone not reaching the required standard in the year-end exams would have to take that year again. I knew if I failed I would be in dire financial trouble, not to mention the chagrin, but many of my peers had no such threats looming over them. Most of them were born into the sort of wealth that left them with no real impetus to graduate at all. Some had already taken the same year several times, preferring the lure of champagne parties and weekend sojourns to London or Paris.

Out of a thousand students, I seemed to be the only one

entering private education for the first time. There were assorted European aristocrats, children of politicians, and princes from the Middle East. A student car park would normally be littered with old bangers and bicycles, but ours boasted hand-me-down Porsches or BMWs, even a discarded Ferrari. Anything less sporty, like a fashionable four-wheel drive, was usually brand new, straight from the showroom. My peers thus did not feel like peers to me at all: they were pampered and primed for a society I had only seen in films. Immersed in the company of those who had more than they even knew, let alone knew what to do with, I became preoccupied with hiding my own perceived inadequacy.

I was not a brilliant student, but won top marks through diligence. In the evenings I studied. I studied at the weekends. In the holidays I went back to York, taking my studies with me. While most people were enjoying their freedom for the first time, I was generally in the library. Unknown to me, Tom was prowling around the campus in his scruffy red *Ford Cortina*, himself unsure whether he would do me harm or good if he found me. Had I not been so studious – instead dallying in the streets and cafés – I might have found out, but I never saw him and he never saw me.

6

Spinach in Bangkok

Nēti nēti
Not this, not that.
What, then, do I need?
I need God's Forgiveness-Heart on earth
and God's Satisfaction-Eye in Heaven. [6]
—Sri Chinmoy

At the end of university sat a very big void. I assumed the world would be clambering over itself with job offers for someone who had a First Class Honours Business Degree. All I knew was that I wanted to be in London, as that was surely where the money lived. The rest of my future was a tantalising mystery, bursting with untold wealth and well-deserved success.

The reality was a very small room in a grey and featureless house, almost falling off the north edge of the underground map. The road was next to Wembley Stadium, so the rough land that posed as our garden filled up with beer cans and chip wrappers at weekends. My three new housemates had surrendered themselves to the gloom of survival in various unpleasant professions, offering no more than a clipped greeting as we passed in the corridors.

Having used the last of my inheritance in trying to keep pace with my university friends, I resolved to take whatever job came first, just as a 'temporary' measure. In the talons of recession, 'temporary' turned into eighteen months. After a brief post, filing documents in Paddington Station, I was Department Assistant for *Menswear (Shirts & Ties)*, in a fashion buying office.

My duties officially revolved around historical sales and stock analysis. I also fetched the tea, did the photocopying, ran personal errands, and took the blame for whatever went wrong. I was paid four-fifty an hour for eight hours a day, but it was polite to work an extra four hours a day for free. *Menswear* was a maze of movable cubicles in a disused ballroom: a large round windowless space, buzzing with tension and telephones.

I was only one insignificant molecule in a thick paste of bodies, oozing into the underground, and discharging itself into Victoria Street every morning, then squeezing back the other way at night. Throughout two years of intensive study I had beaten my mind far beyond its comfort. Although my new job was technically simple, my brain trundled along like a leaning wheelbarrow, dribbling its cargo on the way. There seemed to be neither time nor money for relaxation or creativity, yet I was surrounded by unbearable temptation and unreachable opulence. My health and happiness were draining away, but I knew the only direction was forward, so I patched everything with coffee, alcohol and pharmacy drugs.

Three lads from my degree course had moved into a swanky flat in Finsbury Park, and I craved their familiar company. To numb the pain of aloneness, I began digging myself a steep ditch of debt, drinking and dining out with them in Chinatown late into the night. Sometimes I tagged along to the races if one of them had a horse running, or visited other friends at military college when there was a ball. Debrett's *Etiquette and Modern Manners* was my only companion before any formal event. I feverishly memorised the rules of different cutlery, of when and how to stand or sit, of when and how to write a note of acceptance or thanks, and of what on earth to wear in a given situation. Although manners are based on common sense, at the highest level they seemed to me almost incomprehensible; certainly more complicated than anything I had learned at university. Despite my best efforts, I was always a fumbling bundle of nerves – afraid my cover would be blown and that everyone would know I did not belong. My obvious discomfort was enough to disclose me as a social interloper anyway, even if I did everything by the book.

My brother was at university on the edge of London, so he sometimes met me on Saturdays. We would amble around the city, shopping and reminiscing. His easy company and ready laughter were both a relief. Running was one thing he took very seriously though, and he competed for a local athletics club. I had noticed a specialist running shop in one of the hidden passages near work, so I dropped it into conversation, feeling very clever to have discovered a secret treasure.

'Everyone knows *Run and Become*,' he scoffed. 'I get stuff from them by mail order all the time.'

I felt silly enough not to bring it up again, but I sat on the lawn outside it sometimes at lunchtimes, to catch a rare glimpse of sun. Quite sure I would not belong in such a special shop, I never went in, or even dared stop to look in the window.

At work, I befriended the Department Assistant for *Menswear (Leisure & Casual)* in a nearby cubicle. She was called Clara. We snuck to the canteen together whenever we dared, for instant coffee in plastic cups and high-speed chain-smoking, grumbling and fuming over our powerless state. Clara shared a house in Brixton, which was at least on the same underground line as work, so I often stayed with her overnight. Pungent and electric, its West Indian atmosphere served to lift my spirits from the grey doldrums of Wembley Park.

Clara was genuinely obsessed with clothes, and was thus probably qualified to succeed in the merciless world of London fashion. I made the mistake of borrowing a few items from her wardrobe, and liked too much the attention I drew in the street and in the office. I thus became hooked on labels I could not afford, and ran up a shocking tab on my company store card. We were not compatible friends, but thrown together by circumstance we at least grew to depend on each other.

Jaded from the commute, I decided to move nearer work. I was already hopelessly in debt, so the increase in rent seemed insignificant. Clara offered to join me, so we found a garden flat together at Oval, a luxurious thirty-minute walk from the office. The garden was really a strange-shaped concrete yard. There was a single pear tree at the end that only ever gave birth to a single strange-shaped pear. The floors were made of tawny old wood and the ceilings were high; the walls were a patchwork of thin orange and yellow paint. We listened to moody jazz, drank good coffee and smoked fat French cigarettes.

Clara was not fond of eating, preferring to stay bony like the catwalk models. She had something of a stoop, and was not tall anyway, so her arms and legs looked like those of a child, and her face looked too big for her body. Apart from coffee and cigarettes, she mostly lived on wine and lager, but would tear the corner off anything I was eating and nibble at leftovers, the resulting hunger leaving her whiny and irritable. Both our habits and health grew worse daily. Our coats would not come off at home until we had opened at least a stubby from the fridge. We shopped for clothes on Saturday afternoons, having had only wine spritzers for lunch, which added further catastrophe to our burned out bank accounts. Friday and Saturday nights were only for clubbing. We splashed out on cocaine and spirits if we had just been paid, or slummed it on speed and beer in bleaker times. I took to smoking increasing quantities of weed by myself in the week, sometimes even on my walk to work.

It was obvious by then, that whatever the grade, a degree is not enough for success; either the winds of luck need to be blowing in a successful direction, or one has to hunger for it with every thought. Even then it cannot be guaranteed. Having spent three years near those who had attained worldly wealth or social standing, I knew for certain that neither would be enough for me anyway. I wanted sufficient money to be comfortable, but those around me seemed willing to sacrifice their happiness, their health, and seemingly their very souls for as much money as possible, so as to gain a sense of belonging. If earning money just provided a means of dulling the pain that arose from earning money, I decided it would not suit me. I was already a part of the greater machine though, and did not know how to free myself. I only blundered onward, blinkering my vision with fleeting pleasures.

I was glad to have inspected a fast life first hand; I had always wanted to experience the world for myself, even if some of it was cold or ugly. I was not sure if my father would see it so philo- sophically, having spent a small fortune on my degree, but I had gained more than academic knowledge: I had proven to myself for the first time that if I wanted to reach the highest standards, I could do so. Determination and one-pointed focus could surely be transferred to anything, once I found something I really believed in. By a process of elimination, my ideas of what that might be were quickly running out though. I had ignored God far too long to even know where to find Him, let alone dare ask Him what I should do.

I knew only that I had to pull myself out of the London quicksand before it swallowed me. Too many memories were hiding in England, so I resolved again to move abroad. I found an English teaching course that was inexpensive and fairly unofficial, and I had heard there were certain countries that did not care so much for the highest certificates. Once I had some experience, the doors to other places would at least be ajar. I planned to start in Thailand, and work my way through Asia until I discovered somewhere that felt like home. At least in Thailand I would not risk taking drugs, having heard grisly enough stories of imprisonment and hangings, so my lifestyle would automatically be somewhat cleaner and more affordable. I extended my debts, sold all I could, and bought a one-way ticket to Bangkok.

Somehow Tom was on the other end of the phone one night,

as I was dismantling my empty bookcase and packing the last of my things. Apparently he had called my mother, who thought she had fobbed him off with some vague notion about London, but he had eventually found me. It was a different version of Tom: a light and balanced Tom who had stopped drinking, a Tom who had completed a course of therapy for overcoming his childhood tragedies, a Tom who called and politely asked to see me instead of stalking me in a scruffy *Ford Cortina* as he then admitted he had done. I was bound for York the next morning, but I found myself promising to visit Bristol before I left England for good.

'*Bangkok?* Do they have buildings there? Will you live in a hut made of straw?' demanded Candy in her new and pleasant semi-detached house, nursing her new and pleasant second child on one knee. From various others I heard that Bangkok was awful, unhygienic, unsafe, unsavoury and undesirable in every way. I did not take their word for it, especially as none of them had been there.

The trains from York to Bristol were fully booked for the holiday weekend, so my mother took me to a car rental office. Hardly any cars were available either, but one was at least reasonably priced; it was metallic blue with go-faster stripes. The morning was already sticky and cloudless, so I left my shoulders bare and plaited my hair in two thick cables to keep it off my neck. My mother kissed me goodbye. I did not know when I would see her next, but we had long practised our performance of being brave. I usually called home to say I had arrived somewhere safely, but it was well into the evening when I recounted the crash. Everything had changed – or rather I had changed. In those seeming hours of spinning, I had glimpsed a possibility. I knew some other life was there, somewhere in the deeps of consciousness, but it would take a while to show itself again.

'Live with me,' Tom said that night when I came in from the

deck, bathed in my own grateful tears and the light from the stars. 'Go to Thailand for a few weeks or months if you have to, but come back to me. I only straightened myself out for you. I need you. Nothing makes sense without you.'

'Yes,' I said, dazzled by the miracle of my new life. The word dripped from my mouth like honey from an overfilled spoon; there was no catching it or putting it back. Like a curse or a spell, I knew my fate was sealed by that tiny intractable act of speech. At that moment I did not mind where I lived – I was only happy to live at all.

* * *

My father had worked in Thailand, so he surprised me with enthusiasm for my trip. He knew of a lady called Gail, who loved to take in guests, as long as they had a reference of the sort my father was happy to provide. Instead of a hot and dirty hostel, which was all I could have afforded, I had the maid's room for free in Gail's air-conditioned apartment: hers did not live in as most maids did.

Still euphoric from the previous week's events, I fell hopelessly in love with Thailand, especially Bangkok, and felt almost instantly at home. Nothing could repel me. The scents of drying fish or the aromas of open drains were only parts of a greater mystery, and were thus enchanting. I lived for three months in a state of wonder and thankfulness, a newborn child in a full-sized body, fervently exploring a world I had so nearly left behind on the westbound M5. My daily meditation was resumed in earnest after that abrupt reminder. I did not smoke at all, and only drank an occasional glass of wine with dinner, which I thought very grownup.

It was the start of monsoon, and the most extreme flooding for two centuries. Everything seemed to carry on as normal, just at a slower pace, and with rolled up trousers. Shops stayed open, only they did not make use of the lower shelves. I preferred to travel by river bus, whose service was uninterrupted: it was the fastest way to anywhere, and my favourite haunts – the temples – were never far from one bank or another. It was all part of the adventure wading knee or thigh high to the jetty through what was normally a boat terminal; discovering the hard way where each type of boat did and did not stop, and on which side of the river. No direction can be the wrong direction on an adventure anyway. Wat Pho was my favourite place in all the city: a twenty-acre site with many elegantly-spired temple buildings, and over a thousand images of Lord Buddha. The largest statue reclined a hundred-and-fifty feet long, painted in gold. He lay in such a small house, that just peeping through the door was exquisitely overwhelming. I imagined he had walked in there at human height, then expanded to fit the room in a huge golden bliss, and stayed ever since, smilingly in repose.

I took a Saturday job teaching English to reluctant children, but most of my work was for employees of a Japanese motorcycle company. I loved the people more than anything in the city: their fine features, shining smiles and refined etiquette. Ironically, the country believed by my kinsmen to be frighteningly unevolved, I found to be far more civilised than my own, at least in the qualities that mattered most to me. In sweetness, happiness, diligence, nobility and spirituality, I found them centuries or even millennia ahead of us.

Gail soon took in another British girl about my age, with whom I would need to share my private dominion. Her name was Harry, short for Harriet. She was strong built and her eyes wide set; she wore gaudy colours and rough fabrics. I found her rude and rambunctious, especially compared to the graceful Thais. She would rib me about anything, and took particular exception to my vegetarian beliefs, thus renaming me Spinach. The whole routine reminded me too much of school, and the best I could do was ignore it. By the time Harry arrived, I knew the city well, so it was my natural duty to take her on excursions and explain the idiosyncrasies of public transport. As that knowledge had been hard earned, and as Harry seemed far less than grateful, I begrudged her every moment, but Gail's dogged goodness inspired me to continue nonetheless.

Within a week, Harry softened, or maybe I just grew used to her. I realised she was just as daunted by the whirl of the city as anyone would be on first arrival, and her abruptness was her way of breaking the ice with strangers. It did not have a direct translation in my own inner language, so I took a while to understand. In fact she was warm-hearted, generous and adventurous. Most significantly, she had come to Asia seeking some deeper meaning to life, just as I had. When I first took her to Wat Pho she dissolved in tears of wonderment. From then I knew we could conceivably be friends.

At the back of Harry's travel journal were pages of carefully scribed sayings, chants and poems from all the world religions, collected over many years. On a new page was a single entry:

'Nēti nēti – Not this, not that.'

The line at once catapulted my thoughts into motion, and cleared the stagnant mists of my mind. That simple phrase made sense of my own search for an ever-elusive home. I had moved house as many times as I had lived years on earth, reinventing myself at every turn, but all I knew was that nothing so far seemed to fit. *Not this, not that*: neither a perfect man, nor his family bookshop; neither a Caribbean retirement, nor an expensive education; not children or wealth or fame or social standing; not Britain, and suddenly not really Asia either. I confided all of it to Harry, and she listened as if with her whole being.

'There's still a man in England. I don't love him, but I can't forget him either. Whatever I do and wherever I go, he is still in me, and I don't know why. When I walk away from anything or anyone else, each door closes behind me, but his door keeps blowing open.'

'Well, Spinach, you'd better go back and find out what it means.'

'Damn. I know.'

I called Tom from an elderly payphone in a corner shop. He seemed grainy and distant like a faded photograph, but I assumed it was only a bad line. I told him I had seen all I needed of Thailand, and was coming back soon, just as I had promised. I felt heroic. His tender plea from the night of the crash turned endlessly in my thoughts like a mantra: *I need you, I need you.*

'Right, I'll meet you at Heathrow,' he said, 'just let me know when.'

My spare earnings totalled enough for a final week's sightseeing with Harry. We took a twelve-hour bus ride south to Krabi, then a boat to Ko Phi Phi: an impossibly perfect group of islands. We shared a hut woven from the leaves of coconut, propped on stilts in the pearl-white sand: probably the sort Candy had pictured me living in. We walked barefoot, washed in sea as clear as glass, and let the sun absorb our troubles.

At dinner on our last evening, the stars looked near and brilliant, like pinholes in a velvet canopy that I could almost stroke with my fingertips if I reached. A crab ran across the tops of my feet, prodding me with bony claws. A kitten chased after it, following the tracks exactly with sharp paws. I remembered then that life is really a game: innocent, engaging and always unexpected. Finally I felt ready to play in earnest.

7

The Inner Guide

O Lord Supreme,
Reject me not into the world again.
I have suffered, I am still suffering.
With each breath I breathe,
Fires of wild destruction enter into me.
O Lord Supreme,
Reject me not into the world again,
I pray, I pray, I pray! [7]
—Sri Chinmoy

My hair was scraped back in two high black bunches. I had bought my trousers on the beach: they were black too, tied at the waist, wide at the bottom and wrapped round each leg like a twin sarong, so the sides gaped and billowed. My shirt was a size too small on purpose, in a counterfeit designer label. Fifties-style eyeliner swept out against my sun-weathered face. Every bag and pocket was searched at customs, but I smiled throughout, imagining Tom's grin of relief when he finally saw me.

There was something wrong. I could tell straight away. Everyone else looked towards the sliding slit of the door that dispatched passengers like letters through a post box. Everyone else hoped I was someone they loved, but Tom was looking at his shoes. Apparently I was not needed. I was not even welcome.

'You can stay at mine if you like, until you get yourself sorted,' he offered breezily in the car, after some awkward small talk. 'My housemate won't mind for a couple of weeks. Where are you going to work?'

I did not say anything. My mind was a swarm of angry questions, like a toppled beehive. Indeed, where would I work? Where would I live, more to the point, if he would not have me? And why would he not? I could not have done anything wrong, as I had not even been there. Everything had gone according to my plans and promises in fact, and I was unaware that anything had changed. The people who had shown me kindness in Thailand passed before my mind in a parade of smiles, and I ached to be with them again.

It was the start of winter. The sky wore a coat of steel and the wind was sleety. Hot tears washed the eyeliner down my cheeks. I had less than no money: only a huge pile of debt from before, and no way to increase it or pay it off without a job. I had no friends and no family nearby. I had barely any belongings, not even a warm jacket. After two weeks I would have nowhere to stay, and even those two weeks looked unbearable if I was not welcome. I wondered whether to ask my mother if she would take me back again, but somehow I knew my fate lay ahead of me in Bristol, and there was no option but to face it. I had never felt such a keen and complete sense of destitution. It came without warning or apology, like the sleety winter wind.

'I thought you wanted me to live with you,' I muttered eventually, trying to steady my voice enough to make it sound impartial and workaday.

'I'm not ready. Maybe in a couple of years or something.'

'Why didn't you tell me before?'

'I didn't know before.'

So that was that. The car pulled up on a blank-looking street in Southville, and Tom opened a door in a blank-looking wall. The inside was dim and cold and smelled like burned toast. I was told to put my things under the stairs. Fishing out a towel and some clean clothes, I went up and locked myself in the bathroom. The phone rang below, and Tom was speaking in a kindly voice – a voice he used to save for me – but I did not try to make out the words.

'We've got to go out in half an hour,' he bellowed up through the stairwell.

Who is 'we?' I wondered. *Who is he to say I have 'got to' do anything?* After scrubbing off the blackened tears, I gave myself a defiant look in the mirror, meaning: *don't you dare lose it, you're all that's left.*

'Freya's heating's broken.'

'Who's Freya?'

'A girl I used to go out with.'

'I didn't know you could mend heating.'

'I'm not going to mend it, I just thought it'd be nice to keep her company, she sounds a bit down.'

A bit down. Was this all some kind of elaborate joke, or fantastical dream? At the mercy of shock, I followed like a lamb, but inside I was a tempest. Freya was half-Swedish, as Tom made sure he told me several times. She was blonde and tall and pretty in an obvious way, with speech that slowed towards the end of all her sentences like a clockwork toy unwinding. Sometimes she would trail to a halt even before the end, leaving her mouth hanging open in a vacant question. I stared in silence as Tom talked more within five minutes of entering Freya's chilly lounge than he had done all the way in the car from London. After half an hour, Freya said how nice it was to meet me, and the three of us were suddenly going to the pub. Still they talked and I stared. Tom seemed in an unusually generous mood, buying one round after the other; apparently his vow to stay off drink had lasted about as long as my own. He was downing double bourbons too fast, which I knew would make him combative, but I was matching him, shot for shot. At last Freya left, and we were walking home: Tom's home, not mine.

'What the *hell*?' I opened, knowing after so many drinks I would get a straight answer. I blocked his path, facing him squarely, my eyes boring into him.

'I think I'm still in love with her.'

'I can see that.'

'I thought it'd be interesting to be in a room with both of you at the same time.'

Interesting. No more words had a chance to arrive before my instinct boiled over. In one fluid movement I made my hand into a tight little ball, raised my middle knuckle slightly, swivelled my wrist, tucked my elbow back and shunted the customised fist up into the base of his nose. The knuckle hit between his nostrils with machine-like accuracy. It felt like enough, just for a moment: the cracking sound seemed to right a lifetime of wrongs. In a deserted patch of dockland, I should have been frightened of what he would do to me, but his reaction was fittingly bizarre.

'That was an. Un. Believable. Shot.'

'I know. You deserved it.' I countered calmly, like an automaton.

'I know... but it was... a good shot. Specially for a girl.'

'Thanks.'

We were both laughing nervously then, as though equally surprised and afraid of each other. Nothing was broken and nothing bled. Nothing else happened, except his whole face stayed numb for a week, so he talked as if he had just been to the dentist. There is never any excuse for violence, but no other response seemed available on that day. It was the only time I ever hit anyone. Nobody had taught me how, but as the saying goes: necessity is the mother of invention.

The laughter soon wore off, so did the shock and so did the bourbon. The next day Tom was distressed, and began acting increasingly strangely. Eventually he melted into tears and admitted remorse that I had come back for him, as he had begged me to do. Faced with the reality of keeping any commitment to me, he simply crumbled. Freya was really nothing to do with anything; Tom was just a victim to his own private wretchedness, to which I was only adding. His gutless sobs would swing to burly anger and back again by the hour, making me worry for my safety.

Although glad to know where I stood at last, the reality of my own situation was only devastating. Unable to bear Tom's presence that night, I went for a walk while the city was sleeping. It struck me all at once then, standing on an empty metal bridge that joined one blank street to another across the river. I was alone more than ever before. Like the most pathetic fool, I had given up everything for someone confused and unremarkable; someone I did not even love, and who did not need me. I cried like an infant, and thought I would never stop. My lungs wrung themselves out and the breath did not have enough chances to get back in again. I bent and crouched and finally sat on the cold ground like a beggar, howling into my hands.

Words came then, as if from nowhere and everywhere at once.

'I just want to go home,' I said out loud, 'God, please let me come home, I can't bear it on earth a moment longer. I know I've made too many mistakes and You've given me so many chances and warnings and I didn't pay attention and You're probably very angry. I can't even hope You'll forgive me, or love me, or even look at me, but please let me come home. I'll sit in the smallest corner and I won't say a word, I'll never ask You for anything more, ever. Ignore me, despise me, beat me, I won't mind, I just have to be near You. I have to come home. Please. Please.'

The dark river squeezed on slowly below me like tar. Brunel's Suspension Bridge twinkled in the far distance. Outside myself everything was just as before, but my tears ran dry. A tiny flame was kindling itself inside – maybe it was hope or faith, its label did not matter then. I knew only that my game was not over; I had to stand and return to the arena.

In the house that was not my home, I dug out from my case the book Rosemary had given me almost a decade earlier –

Shakti Gawain's *Creative Visualization* – and decided to choose an exercise I had not tried before. Amongst the pages not overly thumbed and bent was *Meeting Your Guide*. My imagination would follow a series of steps: first to create a safe and beautiful place, then to add a being in any form who would offer guidance and wisdom.

I made a white beach as I had seen in Ko Phi Phi. I could feel the sand between my bare toes. The sun was gentle and blotted at the edges. Although I imagined the sound of the waves, a mist surrounded me so I could only see my own feet at the bottom of the loose white clothes I had invented.

After a while, a figure came into focus through the haze ahead. When he reached my side, I turned and walked alongside him. He was an Indian man, not much taller than me, with a shaven head. His smile was barely perceptible, but brought with it a flood of sweetness and warmth. I did not dare look into his eyes: each seemed to contain its own universe. Lowering my gaze instead to my own hand, I saw his hand next to it. His skin was a rich brown, vibrant and luminous with life, yet soft as a baby's. I thought since I had created him, I had better decide what clothes to give him, although the beauty of his face and hand had left me unaware of the rest of him. From then he had the dark ochre robes I had seen the Thai monks wearing.

It was as if he had always known me. I tried to tell him my troubles at first, but words seemed clumsy, and I soon realised they were superfluous: he already knew what I struggled to say anyway. His answers did not come in speech, and so were not answers as such, but like a flower offering its fragrance, he exuded deep wisdom without effort. He stayed with me only for moments, before walking on through the mist. I was left in such peace that I could not move, either in reality or imagination. Instead I drifted into the safe sleep of a child in a crib: the sort of sleep I had barely even glimpsed in childhood. It was only the start of the most turbulent and miraculous year of my life to date, throughout which I would visit my Inner Guide daily.

* * *

I signed up with the same temp agency as I had worked for in London. They already had a perfect position waiting for me that nobody else on their books could fill: I was to manage a clothing outlet in a department store near Whiteladies Road. It would only be for a few weeks over Christmas, but the pay was better than anywhere I had worked before. My predecessor stayed with me for a day to show me the ropes, then I would be on my own.

'I don't suppose you're looking for somewhere to live as well?' She asked in a singsong Irish lilt.

'Funny you should mention it.' I grinned at my improving fortune.

She had moved out of her boyfriend's place after he had become violent from drink, but he had recently 'straightened himself out,' so she was going back there. I secretly prayed for her sake he would keep his word. The newly vacant room was in a penthouse on Royal York Crescent – already my favourite road in Bristol – a long curved terrace of immaculate Georgian houses at the edge of Clifton Village. The flat's primary tenant was known as Bubbles – I never understood why. He was an old school, pinstriped, rugby playing type, who treated ladies like an endangered species deserving of respect and protection. His tradition of providing sanctuary for threatened females always somehow reached the ears of those in the direst need, and those who also fulfilled certain requirements. His sub-tenant must be employed, polite, neatly dressed, not unpleasant to look at, and with a good sense of humour. She must also be prepared to kiss him on the cheek once every Friday evening, and then chat over at least one gin and tonic. There would be no unwelcome advances and no overnight guests. No cleaning or ironing would be required; a maid would come for such purposes once a week.

I was introduced to Bubbles that evening, which happened to be a Friday. He let me off the kiss just that once, but gin was compulsory with immediate effect.

My health had slid even further from its precarious state in London. Although my Bangkok lifestyle was healthier in some ways, the acrid air had taken its toll. Wading around in flood-water and eating from street vendors had probably not done me much good either, so I had collected a list of exotic ailments. They were not serious, and only combined to leave me a little run down at first. Then as my first temp contract ended, my throat swelled to such a painful extent that I had to steel myself to swallow, and sometimes even to breathe. For the following two weeks, I could barely gather the strength to go outside. Routine tests revealed nothing, so the doctor called it tonsillitis. No matter what he gave me for it, I did not recover properly though, even after months. I took a string of simple short-term administrative jobs, and joined a gym to try and build my strength, but anything more strenuous than walking left me desperately exhausted.

The moment I had claimed back my independence from Tom, he decided to 'need' me again. Apparently feeling needed was still my Achilles heel, and feeling unfettered was his. Like a dog to a whistle's call, again I ran to him, even after all I had gone through to extricate myself. There was no excusing my foolishness; somehow he just had the same hypnotic power over me as before. At the mercy of his moods, I felt alternately as weak as a kitten and as mighty as a goddess. I did not tell him where I lived, we just settled into a friendship at arm's length, meeting on occasional evenings. Bubbles did not approve, but as long as I reported back to him at some hour of the night, and did not disclose our address, he grew to accept it.

Tom had fallen backwards into drugs again by then, especially 'E' – the so-called 'Ecstasy'. Like the songs of ocean sirens, their empty promises lured him: the plastic love of E, the doctored

Elysium of LSD, speed's mock dynamism, and weed's counterfeit peace. Wherever he was led, his true feelings were veiled there by darkness, and he could assume they no longer existed. To my shame, I followed into those murky dens. There was no excusing that foolishness either. Despite my earnest plea to God on the metal bridge, and my sincere efforts at meditation, I still only had one foot in the world arena; the other fit too comfortably in the imaginary world of drugs. There I could drown my every thought in the thunder of electric music, and sidestep each sadness in hours of dance. Naturally those habits did nothing for my physical strength, my happiness, my self-esteem or my deeper understanding of anything, but they seemed at the time a way to survive a life on earth with which I was still not fully reconciled. Already of an imaginative and sensitive nature, I was affected by them more powerfully than I could stand, but I continued indulging for several months anyway.

One weekend, as I turned twenty-six, I had an especially difficult comedown from E. Apart from my usual additional intake of speed on the way up and weed on the way down, mysterious additives often found their way into the benign-looking tablets: some because they were cheaper to source, and some because they were more addictive. I will never know what cocktail I had actually taken that night, but it sparked my loneliest horror ever. All my worst dreams combined into one unending sink of violence that sucked me deeper into its bowels. I blacked out on the arm of a chair, and woke drooling and screaming. While crawling to my bed I blacked out again, and woke only to plummet further into that private hell between consciousness and what felt like a hundred concurrent deaths.

For weeks afterwards I was unable to work, unable to bear either stillness or movement, either darkness or the light of the sun. My organs felt shrivelled and dry, like handfuls of autumn leaves. Sleep was the only release for my body, but it only brought fresh terrors to my mind. I confided the truth to Bubbles

– who was very decent about it – then vowed never to touch drugs again. That vow I kept. Tom and I thus finally began to grow more distant, by dint of our different lifestyles.

I was glad to have some perspective on the habits I had renounced. I watched helplessly, and with a knot in my heart, as friends and acquaintances debased their precious lives. Those taking E every weekend repeatedly lost jobs, unable to function properly in the hands of depression and anxiety. They looked pale and stringy and over-cooked, their eyes gradually receding into dark pits of fear and despair. Like me, they believed they were lost and unloved in the world. E was the only route they knew to feelings of euphoria and a sure connection to the people around them. If drink creates a protective layer of numbness between oneself and the world, E emboldens one to embrace it, however fleetingly and synthetically. The motive was understandable, or even admirable, but the price was horrifically high.

I was the lucky one: I was no longer alone. Except during the aftermath of my final drug episode, no matter how wild my outer life, my Inner Guide visited me every day. Sometimes I was too weak to stand, even in my imagination. On such days he just sat beside me, never seeming judgmental or aloof, exuding the same unvarying wisdom. Often I had no transcendent experiences, but his constancy itself was a powerful source of assurance. I no longer felt a burning urge to understand the mysteries of life; it was enough that he knew the answers. I was as a child ensconced in the back of a car, leaving the mechanics of driving and navigation to a parent. Nobody knew about my Inner Guide, and nobody could take him from me. I was certain my secret inner meetings with him, although apparently only conjured by my mind, brought me fortune far outside anything I could have deserved.

My strength improved gradually over time, and I was offered a permanent job with a database company in Bath. It was never quite clear why they had taken me on, as I had barely anything to do for the six months I was there. They sent me on expensive training courses, so I could set up internal systems far more complex than were necessary. I passed the mornings pretending to work, while really playing game after game of *Solitaire*. In the afternoons I would carry out routine maintenance on existing files, which took hardly any time at all. The remaining hours I spent practising and advancing new skills. My window was broad and reached from floor to ceiling. Through it was a green hill with some little stone houses at the top. I watched people there with their dogs, tramping up and down or playing frenzied games together. They formed an ideal of joyous freedom that always seemed to lay an inch beyond my grasp.

At first I felt like a fraud, which by default I was. After a while I became more philosophical, choosing to see the opportunity as Heaven-sent. Not wanting to look such a divine gift-horse in the mouth, I applied for a higher-paid job in Bristol, with a national mobile phone network. The interviewer knew I was barely qualified, and that even my newly honed capacities would be stretched a little too far, but he liked me, so I got the job. When I broke the news to the firm in Bath, they were indignant at first, especially as I was apparently the third person to leave the same position in two years. To atone for my indulgence, I admitted there was hardly any work involved in the job, the level of training was excessive, and the resulting spare time led to a wandering professional eye. I spent a day teaching the rest of the company to maintain their own files, thus removing the position from their payroll altogether.

My new office was a pool of waist-high cubicles with nowhere to hide. I wore my hair long and sleek; I dressed in fashionable skirt-suits and high-heeled shoes. My days were flurries of meetings and hours of fretting over code. The life did not fit me at all: I was in disguise, like a little girl playing dress-up, but I continued the game anyway. Often my boss would bring me into high-level presentations as a technical expert.

Although I froze with panic at first, I learned to follow blindly after a while, with no plans or notes, but only an open mind. Somehow when a stranger in a suit and tie swivelled towards me with questions, words would come evenly from my mouth like water from a tap: words I did not know were in me, sufficiently convincing words that made people think I knew what I was doing. It was a white-knuckle ride, but I knew just to stay buckled into my seat and go with it.

Traffic after work was always slow. The car parks would empty all at once, leaving stagnant clots in the roads and roundabouts. My elderly white hatchback disclosed me as the new girl, vying for space with a shiny saloon or a sporty coupé. I still had a few select cassettes from my clubbing days which I saved for such times: nothing too raucous, only the ambient tunes and feel-good voices that had no meaning at all, yet lulled me into a familiar comfort. Autumn was drawing her russet curtains. The streetlights blazed new orange against an indigo sky, and I watched the headlamps sweeping past in all directions. Suddenly I entered the same profound beauty as I had felt in the surfers' car: everything blended into perfect synchrony, following a predetermined choreography, like some huge open-air ballet, or a mass of tiny blood cells journeying with purpose through a web of veins.

Where am I going? I wondered. *Not where am I going in my car when I finally get off the slip road of the M5, but where am I going after that, and after that, and after that? More to the point, who am I? This working self is not me; she's no more than a cassette on repeat, turning over again and again at the end of each day. That's enough for some people. Are they more fortunate then, or am I?*

It was all very well to play dress-up, to have a job and a car and a company mobile phone. I was even considering buying a flat, but I knew for me all those things combined would only make a means, not an end; they were a way to live, not a why. There was no instant route to my lasting happiness, I had tried everything to my satisfaction and finally I was sure. How could I expect fulfilment from a person or a pill anyway? Where would be the game in that? No, even my scant society with God left me in no doubt that His Games would have more guile to them; His Play would have more twists to its plot. I had tried a whole catalogue of apparent shortcuts, but they had all ended in cul-de-sacs. There was one road left untrodden. Until then it had looked like the longest and most arduous route of all, but if it actually led me home, it was suddenly worth pursuing, however steep and stony.

I remembered the taste of good Italian coffee in my London flat, brewed at the expense of time and a good deal of mess, compared to the sort that came out of machines in the office at the press of a button. I remembered walking to art school, through the windy winter, over hills and heaths: how much gladder I was to reach the rich warmth and to toast my hands on a radiator, than if I had gone by car. I remembered the nickels my father gave me as a child for being good: how much more I valued them than I would a dollar bill given all at once for no reason. Of course God as the ultimate Parent could give happiness for the asking, just as my father could have given a handful of dollar bills, but at the age of five would I have known its value, or would it have looked to me just like a wad of grubby green paper?

8

Stop, Look and Listen

When I look at myself
I forget to learn.
When I look at the world
I learn to listen.
When I look at God
I listen to learn. [8]
—Sri Chinmoy

It would take more than reading a book. I had enough experience of study to know any real headway would require peers for company, as well as someone to explain things in speech: someone who really knew what they were talking about, who could give examples and answer questions, not someone like me bluffing my way through a technical meeting at work. Looking for an outer manifestation of my Inner Guide did not even occur to me – he surely only belonged in my imagination. Ordinary human beings would do fine, as long as they knew a little more than I did.

I picked up a local magazine I had seen on the counters of bookshops and cafés. After some singles columns and strange poems, ads for pubs and jobs and churches, festivals and foreign films, crystal healing and space clearing and Kung Fu, was a tiny coloured photograph of an Indian man. Under it in tinier type was: *Meditation Course at Clifton Library. Based on the Teachings of Sri Chinmoy. Free Entry.* It was due to start that evening, in the next road from my own, but still I was not sure my efforts would be well invested.

Maybe I should do my laundry instead, I thought. *Actually I think I'm getting a cold. Maybe I'll go to the next one. It'll probably finish late as well, and then I'll be tired for work. So maybe I'll just go for the start and see what it's like. Or maybe not.*

Unknown to me at the time, the advertisement was unique: the only one placed by the Sri Chinmoy Centre in that magazine for years before and after. If I had waited for the next time, it would not have arrived, and I probably would not have remembered the name well enough to pursue it further. My real hurdle was shyness, not laundry. Despite all my life experiences, in new social situations I was straight back in school, longing to be invisible but instead sticking out like a traffic cone. To avoid getting too comfortable at home, I forced myself to go straight from work, intending to perch somewhere discreet like a bird on a fence, with the option of flying off again.

Anxious not to be late, I inadvertently got there half an hour early, and tried to creep in silently at the back of the crowd. Creeping silently is not so easy in high-heels, and the attempt itself proved fruitless anyway: the room was empty except for two fellows about my age. They had just begun setting out the chairs, so the only ones available were at the front. I twisted my mouth into something that was supposed to be a smile. The two fellows had already produced their own smiles easily. One of them handed me a sheet of writing, which I clung to as if for my life, glad just to have an occupation. Folding myself as small as I could into a chair, I glared down at the page. Reading was out of the question; I could only let my heart thunder on, while my own inner hope repeated itself like a mantra: *please don't talk to me.*

At least the room had filled up once the class began. Having sat still for half an hour though, I was already wrestling with the urge to stand, or at least to wriggle around. I thus became more absorbed by my plastic chair than by meditation, wondering if the designer had ever sat in its prototype for more than a few moments. On top of a desk was a larger version of the photograph I had seen in the magazine: a smiling Indian man who was apparently Sri Chinmoy. There was another picture, but as it faced slightly away from me, the light reflected on its surface so I could not see it clearly. Still cringing with shyness in my front-row seat, I did not pay much attention to anything outside myself at first. I tried to listen as an exercise unfolded, but caught my eyes studying a tape mark on the painted wall instead, and began wondering what had been fastened there. Then I pondered how the speaker came to wear that particular shirt on that particular day.

It was explained that the mind, although a useful tool for life on earth, does not know how to find peace. By diving into the heart during meditation, we can let the mind rest from its constant chatter, thus renewing our inspiration and energy. In truth I dared not study the contents of my heart as the exercise required, for fear they would either be too plain or too intoxicating. *What will I do tomorrow?* Asked my mind instead. *What would I have done yesterday if...?* The carpet was thin and cheerless, the light was grey and flickering, the speaker spoke and the chair grew in stubbornness. Musical instruments were carried in from one side.

Lungs know air without cerebral confirmation; they drink their fill instinctively. Leaves know the sun, and stretch their bellies out to it. So it always was for me with ripe berries, or my mother's baking: every cell of me said *yes!* to them with complete abandon. Each is an elemental response, a recognition of source, an ancient resonance beyond the mechanics of questioning. So it was with that music. I thought I had known beauty. I knew I had heard music – reams and reams and reels of it – but it had never reached such depths in me. Seated on the floor, with voice and simple Indian instruments, the two young Englishmen offered Sri Chinmoy's Bengali songs. The words meant nothing to my own English ear. Perhaps one string was too tight, or a note stumbled here and there, but that meant nothing either. I only knew my heart and that music, in an endless now. It seemed there was no mind to demand, and no body to take requests. I knew no imperfection, no bounds within or without, but sensed my own self with sudden clarity and certainty. Tears cascaded to my easy smile. Of all places, in that uncomfortable plastic chair, I was free. I was meditating.

At the end of the class, people left or milled around, drinking the juice and nibbling the biscuits the two young men served – as if they had not already given enough. I did not move or speak for some time, but eventually noticed a table of books. There were prices on handmade labels, so I knew they were for sale. I wanted to buy one to show my gratefulness, and to have some means of encouragement at home, but suddenly remembered I was shy, and scuttled out the door instead. I slept like an infant as soon as my head touched the pillow, just as I had done on the night of the metal bridge. All the world felt safe and yielding.

I returned on one or two more evenings, but outside Clifton Library I forgot too easily the appeal of meditation lessons. Fireworks Night and a couple of dinner invitations easily jostled their way past spirituality in the ranks of my priorities. Sri Chinmoy himself was giving a concert in Edinburgh around that time, and those attending classes were invited to go along. I was baffled that anyone would travel four hundred miles for a musical performance, and did not even consider it.

My initial experience was almost forgotten, but having nothing else to do one day after work, I thought about returning to what I assumed would be some relaxing exercises at Clifton Library. Perhaps they would involve the bloom of a flower or the head of a candle, and maybe some music. I first decided they would be easy once I applied myself, so I did not really need to go. I had a candle and flower in a special place at home, so I could just continue practising at six in the morning and again before bed, as the instructors had suggested. Although I followed all their advice to the letter, my mind wandered more freely at home. At least away from the lure of television and domestic chores I would focus myself more readily, and would probably get a good night's sleep afterwards into the bargain, so I finally launched myself out into the wintry night.

The two photographs were reversed: the smiling one was to the side and the other looked out from the middle of the desk. It was a face in black and white, not immediately recognisable as the same Indian man, but nonetheless a portrait of Sri Chinmoy, known as his Transcendental Picture. The camera's glance conveyed the direct blaze of his eyes in a deep state of meditation. It was explained there is a level of consciousness that transcends all desire and earthly identity, known as God-realisation or self-realisation. This is the ultimate goal of meditation, the highest level of self-discovery: conscious awareness of one's own unity with God. Seen as a game of hide and seek, the world is God's camouflage, and our part is to find Him. By identifying oneself with someone – or even a picture of someone – who has attained this level of awareness, one can potentially receive or increase any divine quality, as from the boundless Universe itself. One can also gain a closer understanding of God, and a clearer sense of His Presence in the self and in the world at large.

After calming our breath and letting go the tensions of the day, we were invited to rest our gaze on the face, as we had done with a flame or a rose. Like all the techniques we had been taught, this one would employ the heart: not the physical or emotional heart, but the spiritual heart in the middle of the chest, where one feels most joy and identification. I had sensed a tingling there during previous exercises, like the press of many tiny fingers. Sometimes it was more a sweet ache, like the stretch of a bowstring. Even without such sensations, focusing on that area in myself brought a tangible awareness of peace, safety, surety and familiarity. While it was not enough for me to be told a place or practice is safe, the theory corresponded with my own instinct and experience, so I knew enough to trust it. I opened my eyes halfway, but imagined I was looking from the heart, as I had learned.

There you are! I called out in silence. It was him, the very same man, my Inner Guide, right there in a real photograph: the same eyes containing the depth of galaxies, the same almost imperceptible smile. I knew straight away, but the face grew in clarity and affinity, gently yet unmistakably, as if coming to me through a sea haze. With wave after wave of tearful relief I knew I had found home at last: it had been inside my own heart all along. I did not want the feeling to end, for him to disappear again as though back into the mist. Could he not stay with me always? Even at the close of the exercise, my eyes refused to leave that face, as dear and familiar as my own. Anger nipped me suddenly: anger at myself. Why had I not gone to the concert in Edinburgh? I would gladly have travelled such a short distance to see him. Who could tell when he would come again, if ever?

People were milling about, drinking juice and nibbling biscuits. At last I could not let my own shyness shackle me. Hungry for the outer words of my Inner Guide, I bought a book called *Meditation: Man-Perfection in God-Satisfaction*. I searched the table for a copy of the photograph to take home, but there were none to be seen. My bravery was already exhausted in the first transaction, so I dared not ask further. It was the last evening of the course. Those wanting to continue could meet the following week at a café – one of many private businesses known as Divine Enterprises, run by disciples of Sri Chinmoy around the world. I felt sure the photographs would be for sale there, displayed on shelves in various sizes.

Yes! repeated itself in me each time I turned a page in my new book. Sri Chinmoy's explanations of seemingly inexplicable spiritual mysteries matched inner inklings that were already my own; his concepts seemed perfectly blossomed versions of closed buds in myself. Even his writings on God – the taboo subject of my childhood – were clear yet poetic, simple yet profound, all without the dryness of a scientific mind, but only a vast heart, at once far sweeter and more compelling than any intellectual argument. Of all the names for God, I learned his favourite was 'Supreme', conveying a state of constantly transcending perfection instead of some fixed height or depth. Depending on the individual mission of each soul, I learned that many different roads could lead to that one ever-evolving goal. A Guru – literally one who illumines, one who destroys darkness and ignorance – is one who can lead to that goal, as he has already made the journey himself. A God-realised spiritual Master's ascent is complete; he has reached the summit. Thus freed from desire, he lives only for those still climbing.

Rather than teaching me spirituality like a foreign language, Sri Chinmoy's words and even his very existence, were reminding me of it all in myself, as if it only lay under lifetimes of forgetfulness. I was like an ancient vessel, buried in the earth for many ages, that he was lifting up and polishing, only to bring out its original lustre and fill it with clear water again.

* * *

A year since I had returned to England, the air held the sparkle and suspense of Christmas. Bubbles had moved to a house in Bath, and I found a flat off Whiteladies Road with a girl from work. Alison was round and jolly. Unless she was sleeping she talked constantly: to me, to herself, or on the phone. I often crept around so as not to be seen, but it was not a large flat, so she could easily lasso me with her one-way conversation, even without leaving the sofa or the kitchen table. The entire bathroom was the colour of an overripe avocado, including the carpet, which bothered me more than it should have. Although I still did not have the deposit to buy my own flat, Alison's talking, and a bathroom that never looked clean even when it was, spurred me on to save harder for it than ever.

The café where the classes were to continue was in Montpelier, on the far side of Redland, and far outside my geographical comfort zone. I arrived early and hunkered in the car to see if other people would go in first. The windows were papered with large posters, to block out distractions from the road during meditation. The unknown interior was thus almost more than my shyness could surmount, and I wondered several times whether to just drive away. At five minutes to the start, a figure came in silhouette, tried the door, and disappeared within. Another two came together and did the same. Finally I forced myself to follow.

It was a long thin room, with tables stacked up at one end, and a pale blue rug rolled out at the other. A little English lady sat there on the ground, wearing an Indian sari, and attending a harmonium like the one I had heard in the library. Four or five others were chatting, but they turned to smile and watch me enter. The lady beckoned me to join her, and I practically ran there for cover – it looked the friendliest and least conspicuous place. Behind on a table was the black and white photograph I had thirsted to see again.

I remember none of the words from the talk, but there was music, which we were all allowed to sing: simple songs repeated in beguiling echoes that I did not want to end. The lady made chords that pulled on my heart like the clasped hand of a playmate. Her own voice was clear yet quiet, full of the same happy tenderness I had seen in her eyes. By subtle glances she noted how the music touched me, and we continued for a long time.

Sri Chinmoy was talking and meditating then on a video screen. I was loath to miss an instant by blinking, but my tears gave me no choice. I had never heard my Inner Guide's voice: neither the warmth of it, nor the music of its Indian tones. His clothing made him all the more vibrant and real, yet still other-worldly. He wore an Indian *dhoti kurta* – a long tunic and a separate length of cloth wrapped round the legs and waist. It was in a much brighter shade than the earth colours of a conventional renunciate, and it was satin too I noticed, not cotton. He played an *esraj* – a long bowed instrument I had never seen. The sound seemed to call from another realm, and I wished it would never end. I was like a child first discovering her father is not only her father, but has a whole working life as well: as a doctor, or a janitor, or a watchmaker. I had only really known his silent wisdom up to then, but Sri Chinmoy was a sportsman, a painter and songwriter, a poet and playwright, humorist and humanitarian. He was also a treasured friend to so many more than just me – to stars, royals, presidents and Olympians – people I would never dream of meeting.

The lady had made us soup. She brought out a nourishing grainy sort of bread and lots of butter too. Her kindness was almost more than I could receive at once. Each of the Centre members had a similar robust willingness, and a natural smile, but they were each very different in other ways, like cousins in a wide extended family. We made a long table from a few smaller ones pushed together. Sitting there with a cup of chamomile tea, I realised my shyness had evaporated. I belonged.

On a shelf by the counter were Sri Chinmoy's books for sale, but I could not see the photograph I craved to own. Having been given so much already, I did not dare ask more, but the lady seemed to read me anyway. It would take me some time to realise such meditation centres need different qualities from their leaders than most other organisations do. The lady with the harmonium was the leader of Bristol Sri Chinmoy Centre, but her gentleness and humility had not let that possibility arise in my mind.

'You liked the music didn't you?' Her eyes all but disappeared in a twinkling grin.

'Oh yes! Thank you!'

'You like meditating on the Transcendental Picture too?'

'Oh yes, very much.'

'Let me give you something?' She asked as if it were my favour to receive, not hers to offer. In case I denied her that joy, she had already tiptoed like a sprite down a narrow flight of stairs, and returned with a colour photograph.

'One day you can have your own. This is for you until then.'

Part of me did not dare touch a thing so sacred, but most of me claimed it like a child claiming her father's wealth as her own. It was not a Transcendental Picture – Sri Chinmoy looked halfway between the two photographs I had seen in the classes, as if smiling and meditating at the same time. My next thought had already been anticipated too, and I was handed an envelope in which to keep it safe.

'You choose your own frame, whatever you like best,' she said.

I could only smile. Words seemed coarse and empty. Only music or silence could have said what I meant, but the lady seemed to know.

I did not open the envelope again until everything could be done with due ceremony. The next day I chose a new frame, hand-painted in Persia with little blue buds and green leaves edged in gold. I hoped Sri Chinmoy would like it – next time I saw the lady I would ask her if he might. After bathing and choosing clean clothes, I slid the photograph behind the freshly buffed glass, setting it first in one special place and then another. At last I sat down to meditate, looking into the face from my heart. Sri Chinmoy's smile appeared to broaden, in tandem with my own.

'This is a drop of peace.' I thought I heard him say – inside my heart, not in my ears.

'Only a drop?' I asked in silence. Both our smiles seemed to grow again at my outrageous cheek and greed.

The drop in my heart was like a golden bead of light that grew to fill not only me, but also the space around me – the way a tiny bulb can illumine a room. A drop of peace was clearly more than I could use, at least for the time being. I wore it like a secret garment for the rest of the day.

* * *

A new face appeared at the café one evening; a visitor from another Sri Chinmoy Centre had come to teach us how to blend art with meditation. I had seen a slideshow of Sri Chinmoy's *Jharna-Kala* or *Fountain-Art* paintings. At first I did not notice much in them, but I was only looking with my ordinary human eyes. As soon as I gazed out from my heart the way I had learned, the life in the pictures dazzled me such that I did not want to take my attention from them; I almost did not want to breathe for fear that new and subtle vision might wing away like a startled bird. I wondered then that even for a novice like me, meditation might reawaken my long-lost creativity, and even open new worlds of it.

We wore old shirts back to front like in pre-school, and against my perfectionist nature I was soon daubing a page with multi-coloured paint more freely than I had done since that age. We drew then without viewing the page at all, but only resting our gaze on a flower as if from our hearts. The results were beguiling; seemingly from parts of ourselves we had never tried to use.

I had faith enough that the road of meditation would lead me to happiness, albeit a less glamorous and obvious road than the ones I had tried. Others would have other routes to their own happiness via different paths, but this was my way home. I knew as surely as I could know anything that Sri Chinmoy was my true spiritual teacher. I saw him then as my mountain guide, showing me the swiftest route to my own destined peak, pointing out the shortcuts as well as the pitfalls along the way. Not only was he *a* Master – an expert teacher, such as one would follow for proficiency in music or martial arts – but *my* Master.

It had become a custom for a few of us to stay late into the evening after a class, chatting and drinking tea. Mostly it was a chance for us to glean stories and answers about Sri Chinmoy and his teachings. For my part, I also did not want to leave a place that felt more welcoming than the flat where I actually lived. One night after watching a video of Sri Chinmoy's sporting activities, the conversation turned to running.

'I hate running.' I said without apology.

I boasted then that my strength had mysteriously improved since I had started meditation classes. Although I was no longer obsessive about training at the gym, I had almost regained the same fitness as I had before, just through the enjoyment of it.

'Fitness helps meditation, and meditation helps fitness,' came a gentle response. 'Running is like meditation for the physical; it clears the mind and keeps the body fit, both of which are helpful spiritually. Sri Chinmoy recommends running above any other exercise, as long as you're strong and well enough to run.'

The proviso was not enough excuse for me, as I had just proven with my bragging. I remembered running with my mother every morning: the affinity with nature, the clean exhilaration, the glowing start to the day that no other start could match. I sulked in silence then, knowing it was true. Bristol Half-Marathon was due in May, so I signed up the next day, and went out for a frosty jog.

I returned to the café frequently over the following month, and was welcomed like an old friend, either for lunch at the weekends or at meditation evenings. I knew there would come a time when even those classes would end, but I assumed I could join the Centre then officially. To the six of us remaining at the close of the course, it was explained that indeed we could apply to become one of Sri Chinmoy's students, or 'disciples' as he called them. I would need to write a letter to him personally, and send photograph of myself. By meditating on my picture, he would be able to determine whether or not I was ready for the spiritual life, and if so, whether or not he was meant to be my Guru. I had felt sure of both answers even before I knew his name, but the thought of an outer confirmation thrilled me beyond all hope or expression.

9

Learning to Live

In the dark and dense night,
You cast Your benign Eyes upon me.
Take me and make me Your very own,
Offering Your Compassion.
I am Your innocent child.
Alone do I walk on a thick, dense path.
With Your two Arms, embrace me.
Allow me not to be drowned and washed away
By the turbulent currents of life. [9]
—Sri Chinmoy

In my glee, I did not see the final hurdle, and collided with it quite inelegantly. To reach the finish line of becoming Sri Chinmoy's disciple, I would be required to make a few changes in my worldly habits. Purifying and simplifying my outer life would apparently help me to meditate. It meant avoiding any substances that would harm, agitate, or dull the so-called 'subtle nerves' necessary for meditation. It also meant avoiding the main source of emotional turbulence known to humankind: seeking a partner. All this sounded logical, but these were not only practical changes; they were a way of honouring and sanctifying my commitment to the inner life, just as a monk or nun would take vows on entering an order. Specifically I would need to follow a vegetarian diet, abstain from drugs and tobacco, abstain from alcohol, and – as I was yet unmarried – remain single.

The first two requirements I had already chosen for my own reasons, and the third at least made sense to me. My Inner Guide had stopped visiting me as he used to even after my excesses. Perhaps because I had finally found him in the outer world, his presence on my private patch of inner coastline was no longer necessary. Although meditation came spontaneously if I was sober, it hid or ran off like a deer if I had indulged even mildly, and often my indulgence was far from moderate. I would perhaps not give up the vice of drink immediately, but I could see the reason for trying.

Some part of me balked entirely at the fourth requirement. Tom was pretty much out of the picture, so I already considered myself single for the time being, and I had also run far from the idea of bearing offspring. Still I declared openly that I was 'definitely not ready' for such a holy life, and would 'certainly not be ready' for the duration of this lifetime. That level of commitment was for other people – people with a clear divine calling – not me. I tried to cover the tracks of my own spiritual experiences to date, denying their existence altogether. It was easy to do at first because nobody else knew about them. To others I decided to claim only some vague leaning towards meditation; it was surely just a hobby for me, and did not need to be a way of life. Surely I would need to marry at some point! Who was I to think of becoming the direct disciple of such a lofty spiritual Master anyway, especially having led a relatively coarse existence until then!

There was no escaping the truth for long though. In my heart, the decision had already been made: perhaps as I spun in slow motion on the M5, or maybe before I even entered the world. It just took a little while to filter through to all the other parts of my being. I could not pretend meditation was unimportant to me, not after all I had jettisoned in the quest for truth. The problem came down to the fierce aversion to aloneness that had followed me from birth. I assumed being single would mean being solitary. I could simply not imagine solitude and happiness living in the same sentence.

I pictured myself then as a fledgling on the edge of a nest I had obviously outgrown, but not daring to jump in case my own wings failed me. Leaving that nest went against an instinct of survival, and yet for one who is born to fly, it is the only route to that same survival. There was no point wishing one was born a toad or an antelope or some other ground-dwelling creature, if that was obviously not God's Intention. It was something I had only read about, but I knew it then for sure: there can be two very powerful competing instincts from two levels in one tiny self, such is the guile of God's Game. At last in that light, I saw my resistance as no more than a fear.

Since first practising meditation, my policy with fears had been to go after them and stamp them out, or to at least shake my fist at them before running away. Having stared even death in the face on the motorway, I had felt more alive, but I knew very well that living was not some linear predictable process, complete with a reliable set of instructions. All the props and crutches – of comfort or seeming necessity – had been stripped away on my return from Thailand. After the resulting shock, on some fundamental level I was already clearer and stronger for having faced so many fears at once. Logically I was sure even then that a job or a relationship, any material possession or social position, did not define me. That my sense of self lived on, even in their absence, had formed further proof: categorical evidence for my inner detective.

Although devastating at the time, the turning point on the metal bridge had been a crucial part of my journey. I did not know then, but such complete desolation and annihilation of identity has been a common course for many who have gone before me – across the ages and myriad routes to the one same goal of spirituality. Some call it the 'long dark night of the soul'. It is also said that when the student is ready, the teacher appears. Apparently I was ready: nothing and nobody else stood in my way. Nobody else could make those steps for me either, but

»meone was already leading me through the darkness. It was ike crossing a frail bridge of rope that shook and swayed in the wind, but linked my route to a higher peak. I trembled at the long empty space beneath it, but some lasting ounce of faith bid me walk across. Beyond it, the ground was already firmer than anywhere I had ever stepped.

It took only two days to reconcile myself, but a lifetime seemed compressed inside those hours. I pictured Nanny holding out the seam of her wedding dress with a hand like porcelain. I saw her stumbling then, half carried from her husband's wake to end her own days without him. I pictured my mother on her own wedding day, in sixties satin and a neat little waist, my father in a laddish smile and sideburns; nine years later either he was gone or we were. From any angle the result was the same: we each had to start again. I saw James fading from me behind imagined snow, and felt the cool space in my heart where he used to be. If even he was not enough, who could be? No, I could not expect anyone outside myself to give me happiness – not the real sort that would stand up to weathering. Only God had access to products of such quality.

I allowed my mind the comfort of knowing I could change my course after a day or a year. If in future I suddenly felt sure a man was more likely to keep his promises of happiness than spirituality, I could go back the way I came. What I could not live with was turning away at the start, having never even tried. It seemed even to my mind a practical way to lead a spiritual life: I would still have a home and a job, but would support it all with inner strength and a constant awareness of the divine. It was the first time I had made a clear decision about my life without any influence from friends or family. As my parents had always intended, my spiritual choices were to be made only by myself.

I rummaged in all the best stationery shops for the right pen and paper, but what instruments could possibly fit the task of writing to a spiritual Master? I traipsed through a forest of doubts about my handwriting or my choice of words, but then decided I must be myself, as he would see through any charade. I simply chose what I liked best: a card with a photograph of autumn leaves in all the possible colours, like the ones my childhood self had found under a maple tree. *How could that be wrong? It's God's Art, not mine,* I decided. As my Inner Guide, maybe he would like the same things as I did anyway.

I had a picture taken in a booth near work, in black and white instead of colour. If I liked meditating on his black and white picture more than the colour one, maybe he would have the same preference. The collar of my black wool skirt-suit showed a little at my neck. I had tidied my hair in long straight layers, and wore a little less make-up than usual. The damp strip dropped out of the machine, revealing four wistful copies of me, each with a barely perceptible smile.

On New Year's Eve I drank like a sailor, vowing then never to touch another drop. In the groggy aftermath, I felt sure to keep my promise at last. The one remaining task was to tell Tom, but I thought he would not be interested, having already drifted so far from my world. First he mocked me, but then he showed a jealous sort of curiosity, so I suggested he join the next set of classes at Clifton Library. To my surprise he went, but did not return after the first night, and would not talk about it. That was that, or so I thought.

It was then that Tom fell apart. He had imagined all along I would be there if he finally decided to make a space for me in his life, but I was no longer tethered to his whims. It was clear to me that we must go our own ways, but drugs had further eroded his mind, so for him things were far more complicated. Although I thought I was only a tiny part of his life, to him I was a lynchpin steadying the crooked wheel of his emotions. According to Tom, removing myself was to let him tumble. My old familiar need to be needed opened one eye at the whistle's call, but did not rouse itself to follow. Even before, when things were much simpler, I had not been enough for him, and I certainly had neither the strength nor compulsion to carry him out of that deepening mire. I could only pull myself away or sink into it with him. Either way, I was powerless to help.

Tom inevitably blamed me for the collapse that followed, and even had me worry for his life. Eventually he admitted he needed more help than I could give, and at last he felt bereft enough to seek it. His parents took him into their care in Wales; the doctors gave him strong prescriptions and a regimen of counselling. Knowing he was in safe hands, I closed the door at last. The echoes rang out for a while, but it never blew open again. Tom had apparently played his role in my life's drama, and I had played my role in his. Via some roundabout route, we had actually brought each other to where we needed to be. He had lured me back from Asia on false or imagined promises, by a power much stranger than love. Had I been left with more than just myself to depend on, I would not have longed so keenly for my true inner home. In turn, by removing myself from Tom's world, I left him to seek his own apt refuge. We were each a part of the other's journey, but neither of us could have been the destination.

* * *

The Centre Leader received a call from New York, late on the night of February fourteenth, to say that Sri Chinmoy had accepted me as his disciple. I was due at the café the next morning, so I heard it from her then. At the time I felt just as before, and was not duly surprised at the news, but more relieved to know my convictions had not been illusions. I had waited several weeks for a response, which apparently was not unusual, but to me the date of that outer confirmation could not have been more perfect: St Valentine's Day. It may have been coincidence, but I chose to take it as a sign of recognition from God that I had accepted the challenge of a single life, and as a secret promise that the spiritual life would outweigh the charms of any earthly romance.

Two of us applied and were accepted at around the same time; the second was a Spanish girl studying at university. She was light and wiry like a butterfly, but left a whirlwind of chaos and laughter wherever she went. Everyone loved her, mostly because she loved everyone, but we became especial friends due to our similar circumstances.

We four would meet at the proper Centre from then – on our own particular nights for a while, so as to get used to things before joining the official meetings. The Centre was a converted front room in a house shared by some of the boys. Sri Chinmoy regarded all his male disciples as boys, no matter their age, and the females as girls. To him age was largely in the mind: by dwelling on our increase in years, we only limit ourselves and squander our enthusiasm. By thinking of ourselves inwardly as seven years old, no matter our earthly age or responsibilities, we can retain our youthful happiness and freshness. I liked the idea very much, but childhood felt yet more serious to me than adulthood. My seven-year-old memories were especially grave, mostly revolving around loss and the resulting grief, so they would take some unlearning. The spontaneity of my new Spanish companion gave me hope that my own sombreness might wear off in time, but I would not want all her caprice. I hoped still to carry my sensible and dutiful qualities, but perhaps just in a lighter item of luggage.

It was only when I reached home after hearing the news of my acceptance that I felt its impact. Somehow Alison's chattering and the avocado bathroom were more of a hindrance than ever to the life of quietude and purity I had entered inside myself. I realised I would need to do all I could to maintain a sense of sacredness in my outer life, regardless of whether the people around me understood or valued the same things as I did.

Although mastering the four requirements was a good start, my spiritual self felt like a new flower that needed safeguarding against the winds of the world. Admittedly leading a spiritual life within the secular would be more comfortable in some ways than the cloistered choice of a traditional nun, but in other ways it would be more challenging. I would be immersed in daily disturbance, distraction and temptation.

Nobody asked me to do it; I just thought life would be simpler if I drew a line between my old priorities and my new ones. My fingernails were the first to go. They had always grown easily, so I had kept them long and painted them carefully in the style of a French manicure. I knew I was vain about them, so keeping them would only invite the sort of attention I no longer wanted. To me cutting them was akin to shaving my head. My hands felt bare and short like a child's at first, but I soon welcomed the use of my fingertips after so many years, especially for typing at work or for fiddly things like threading a needle. The eyeliner went the same way as the nail varnish, and so did the lipstick. Photographs of Tom and others from my murkier past followed them all into the bin soon after. There was no sadness at all, only relief. My inner luggage was already easier to carry.

On the night of the art class, I had seen a book by Sri Chinmoy called *Colour Kingdom*, containing his spiritual interpretations of various colours. I was fascinated by all of them and surprised by some, but his views on the colour black I could almost have predicted myself: it apparently represented inconscience. As I was hoping to become *more* conscious by practising meditation, wrapping myself in such a void would only add to the challenge. Although I naturally associated it with death and darkness, I had worn a lot of black since school, because it goes with everything. Then almost everything ended up being black, and there was not much else to go with it anyway, so it may as well have been mint green for all the sense that made. I certainly felt less sombre when I wore my blue suit to work instead of my black ones, so it was not only book knowledge. There was soon a pile of black things for the charity shop, and a few other things that were admittedly flirtatious. I went shopping for happier colours instead, and chose more modest necklines than I would have done before. It seemed years had been shed from my age when only that was done.

The last and most complicated choices concerned my music. I knew that apart from spirituality, music affected me more deeply than anything, so I could not hope to prise my emotions from it, nor would I wish to. After listening to a few albums I was not sure about, I decided to keep anything Classical, because it seemed timeless, and a lot of it was obviously more divine than earthly. One boxed set seemed to form a border of the two worlds: a collection of anonymous pilgrim songs. They were ostensibly songs for God, but some were deliberately written in a bawdy drinking style so as to make 'conversion' more palatable for the masses. With a smile of irony I decided it fitted me rather too well to let it go. The rest had too many recent memories hidden in them, most of which were sad or strange. I sealed the tapes and discs of that sort in a bubbled envelope and gave them to my brother, knowing that way I could borrow them back if I missed them. I had already explained briefly to him and to my mother the changes I was making, but my family was used to me reinventing myself, and probably assumed the spiritual life was another fad, like song-writing or scuba diving. I was fairly sure it was more than that, but after trying out so many versions of myself, even I would have to wait and see before being certain.

* * *

The Centre room felt full of warmth and welcome, but looked like a clear pool in a snowscape. Until then I would have assumed two such very different impressions could not live together in the same place, but they were perfectly in balance there. The carpet was lavishly soft, and powder blue as though reflecting the sky. The walls and ceiling were brilliant white, further brightened by ambient lighting. A Transcendental Picture, much bigger than any I had seen, looked in from the bay of the window on a low white table, making a sort of shrine area. It was set with a long white candle on one side, and on the other a gentle profusion of yellow roses in a bowl. The room itself was otherwise empty, apart from some neat stacks of cushions at the back, some well-ordered shelves of books, a modest stereo, and the scent of jasmine. The rest was apparently to be found within.

The Spanish girl and I arrived early for our first lesson in wearing a sari. My mind resisted, and I said so. Although I thought it slightly odd, I was not so averse to seeing it on other Europeans, but wearing it myself was a different matter. I had no outer connection to India, and had not even been there, so flouncing about in Indian garb felt fraudulent. It was explained that having a special set of clothing for meditation was like having a special area in one's house for that purpose: just another way of creating sanctity, in turn making meditation easier and more enriching. The boys thus wore pure white trousers and shirt; the girls wore a sari of any design or colour, except black. It would take me a while to grow into the theory, and a while longer to claim it as my own, but I agreed at least to try one on. My companion had no such qualms – to her everything was a game, so her life was in many ways more straightforward.

We were shown into a back room overlooking the yard. My new artist friend, who gave the painting class, had sent two saris for me from her own collection. That kindness itself further softened my resistance. After a few failed attempts, stabbing myself with safety pins, twirling one time too many, or wrapping the wrong shoulder, I eventually mustered enough stubbornness to fold mine in place, although not to my own self-imposed standards. The other girl was chattering and flitting about so much she practically had to have hers put on for her, but she looked dainty when it was done; even more like a butterfly. I felt quite regal in mine, and looked much smarter in the mirror than I thought I would, but such comments were kept to myself in case they sounded immodest. Already saris were growing on me: rather than acting like a uniform, they seemed to accentuate different qualities in each person.

The meeting itself consisted of familiar musical and meditative ingredients from our evenings at the café, but each felt magnified by the purity and sanctity of that room. At the end, bowls of tangerines, iced biscuits and squares of chocolate were placed at the front as *prasad* – blessed food. The word was unfamiliar, but the custom I recognised fondly from the little dusty chapel in Mexico. Two envelopes were then put on the low table. To my tearful relief, they contained Transcendental Pictures for us each to take home.

Around that time I had a problem I could not seem to solve, either by talking to others or through my meditation. I do not remember what it was, but I do remember someone suggested writing it in a letter to Sri Chinmoy: not to send, but just to leave in front of my Transcendental Picture at home. I imagined I would have quite a few problems throughout the rest of my life, so rather pessimistically I bought a heavy spiral-bound notebook for the purpose, intending to leave it open at the appropriate page as I went along. I sat down to meditate, then wrote this first problem down. As it was a complicated one, the letter went on to three sides, so I carefully laid book open at the first page, meditated again, and left the room. Then I wondered when the letter would be read – would it take moments, days, weeks? I went back again, vaguely hoping to sense an answer to that simpler question, to discover the first page had turned over to reveal the second and third. The window was not open, so it could not have been a draught, and it is not in the nature of heavy spiral-bound notebooks to do anything other than lay down flat. I took that to mean not moments, days or weeks, but now: whatever the problem and however it is presented, as long as a solution is sincerely sought.

* * *

Each month or so, all the British Centres would gather in one city or another over a weekend for 'Joy Days', where we would meditate together, eat together, run together and entertain one another with musical or humorous acts. There were games too, and a great deal of prasad. It was at the café that I met the members of my extended spiritual family for the first time. The room bustled with more visitors than it could reasonably hold, so some spilled into the stairwell or stood in mirthful bunches, chatting and chuckling, munching on bright salads and home-baked lasagne. We two newcomers were paraded about like twin princesses, pampered with smiles and female attention. I needed a notebook for writing down new people – many were known by spiritual names bestowed on them by Sri Chinmoy. The names were beguiling and beautiful, and had yet more beautiful meanings, but I was as though back in my infancy, frowning and listening long before daring to try the new exotic words for myself.

By chance I settled at a table with a pianist, who had her own music group called *Temple-Song-Hearts*. My artist friend sang in the group and had given me recordings, so I had heard much of their repertoire already and was very taken by it. Although all the songs were by Sri Chinmoy, each had its own distinct atmosphere and personality. Some were pensive and delicate, reminiscent of a lone longing; others were floods of bracing power; others were quickening canons, whose playfulness had me clapping along with joy. I was suddenly shy in the company of one so gifted, even though apparently there was plenty to say.

'Keep your eye on this one,' said the Centre Leader as she passed, raising an eyebrow in my direction, although she was hardly visible under a huge basket of bread, 'she's got a *voice* and an *ear*.'

I was not entirely sure what she meant, but the pianist eyed me more seriously then and quizzed me about my singing experience. I mumbled through it as briefly as possible, quite certain she would not be interested in my music career once she knew how short and unwholesome it had been.

Soon after, most of the Centre flew to 'Celebrations' in New York. For the anniversary of his arrival in the west every April, and his birthday every August, Sri Chinmoy's disciples from all over the world went to meditate with him in person. Two or three from Bristol could not afford the airfare that time, and stayed behind to staff the café. The rest of us would need to wait until we had been in the Centre for a year before we could go, and we all wanted to help keep the café open too.

It was my first encounter with 'selfless service' in the Centre – serving others without expecting any benefit in return, other than the enjoyment of giving. Sadly my waitressing skills had not miraculously improved in line with my fitness. However keen I was to be of use, I was still a menace: in the kitchen or at the tables. I was thanked politely for my efforts, but was only ever invited back as a customer rather than a worker. The only thing I could be trusted with was washing up, but there were always ample volunteers for that. I discovered it had been Sri Chinmoy's favourite job at the ashram, the spiritual community where he grew up. The simple activity left his mind free, so he could easily meditate at the same time.

My brother came to stay for a weekend in May so he could keep me company at the half-marathon. Keeping me company was a loose term: we both knew he would finish in half my time, but it was a comfort to know he would be covering the same ground. Still determined to 'hate running', my road training had been somewhat slapdash. My lungs and heart rose willingly to the occasion, but apparently running needed quite different muscles from the ones I used in gym training, so my legs were buckling by ten miles. I was too proud to walk in a race, so I sort of hobbled and convinced myself it still counted. A stream of stragglers passed me until even the walkers outstripped me one by one. I gave them a knowing grimace, or a weak flap of the hand as they passed. The Portway was usually a busy entrance to the city. A section nearest the river had been closed for the race, but opened again after two hours: not to traffic, but to something far less predictable. There was a complete fairground, with rides and dodgems, clowns and coconut shies. Changing tack even slightly was more discomfort and complication than I thought I could handle by then, but I was suddenly like a character in some bizarre computer game, weaving in and out of bumbling families and clumps of teenagers with cuddly toys and pet dogs and hot-dogs and cold drinks and candyfloss. I felt I had run the length of the country by the time I reached the city again, but had to admit nothing could replace the feeling of crossing that finish line. Despite my initial reluctance and the protestations of my legs, I had caught the running bug.

I was nervous before my first proper Centre Meeting, which was silly since the programme, the place and most of the people were very familiar by then, and since it was supposed to be more about the interior world than the outer one anyway. Those I had not met lavished the four of us with kindness, and everyone had bought us gifts. Apart from the room being fuller than before, and the silent meditation being a little longer, it all seemed the same at first, but a new challenge was about to present itself.

Although I was already of a somewhat restless nature, on our own separate evenings everyone seemed fidgety to some extent, so I was not so conspicuous if I was having a fidgety day. I proudly imagined I could sit still for half an hour of silent meditation if I set my mind to it, but in practice it was not so simple. One leg felt like there was something sizeable crawling inside it, and I yearned with all my being to wiggle it. The same problem had arisen in the past while watching films, but nobody minds or even notices then. Knowing I had to be still made it infinitely harder to do so. My concern not to disturb people was equalled by my fervent desire not to make a bad impression. It was more an exercise in endurance than meditation. I held my breath and felt prickles of sweat growing in my eyebrows; I tried guessing the time and counting out what I thought were blocks of sixty seconds; I tried tightening the muscles discreetly under my sari. Nothing helped – ironically nothing except the chant of *Aum* signifying the end of the meditation.

It happened more often than not after that, but I did not say anything, and there was nothing I could do. I tried all sorts of potions and postures and pills at home, but to no avail. Although meditation was almost impossible at fidgety times, I still felt almost the same afterwards as I did after a good meditation, just by being there with others: singing, reading, and making a sincere attempt to be still. The benefits increasingly outweighed the discomfort, and the discomfort itself gradually abated for the most part. Even on the seemingly unbearable days, I realised there was nowhere in the world I would rather be than in that room, and I always longed for my next visit.

10

The Outer Guide

O Master-Musician,
Tune me for life again.
The awakening of new music
My heart wants to become.
My life is now mingled
In ecstasy's height. [10]
—Sri Chinmoy

Sri Chinmoy's visits to Britain were rare, so I was still smarting from the missed opportunity in Edinburgh, when I heard he was to come back that spring. There would be two concerts: one at the Royal Albert Hall, and one at Christ Church Cathedral, Oxford.

As all of Sri Chinmoy's concerts were free to the public, there was ample opportunity for selfless-service leading up to them: fortunately for me, the sort that required no waitressing skills. I was sure handing out leaflets in the streets and distributing them through letter boxes would need no more than the capacities of walking and smiling, so I offered to go along.

'The leafleting headquarters are at Run and Become. It's a specialist running shop off...'

'Victoria Street?' I interrupted with a frown. Of all the thousands of shops in London, there were few whose addresses I knew so well. 'Why *there*?'

'It's a Divine Enterprise; a family of disciples has been running it since the eighties. How come you know it though? It's tucked away in an alley.'

I could not respond for a while, there were too many *but*s and *what if*s colliding with one another in my head. For a year and a half I had worked over the road from a Divine Enterprise – one of only two or three in England at the time. If I had gone inside I would have seen a picture of Sri Chinmoy, but would I have felt anything, not having yet met him in my inner world? There was no knowing, and it did not matter by then, but the coincidence was breathtaking.

Although the shop was in central London, the undeniable energy on the street outside seemed dull and drained compared to the vivacity of Run and Become. Sri Chinmoy looked out from a poster taped onto the glass entrance. Inside I already felt I belonged. Some faces were familiar from the Joy Day, and others were introduced from behind towers of shoeboxes or folders of charts and figures. I had probably passed them in the street three years previously, or stood behind them in a queue at the supermarket, or sat with them on the underground. In a strange way that thought was a comfort: at a time when I had felt especially lost and bewildered, I was all along surrounded by my future friends. In my days at the fashion buying office, I would have been terrified of meeting the owner of such a seemingly elite establishment, but in reality he was all smiles and booming laughter. I felt far more special when I left than when I had come in, just for being included in his vibrant attention. It was obvious everyone loved him and seemed to revolve around him, while he spun in the centre of it all, steadfast yet radiating childlike enthusiasm.

By chance while in London I ended up sitting in on a *Temple-Song-Hearts* practice, or at least I thought it was by chance. Immersing myself in that luxurious sound I could not have been happier, but to my astonishment the pianist then asked me to stay behind afterwards for tea. The other girls gave me kind but mischievous smiles as they left: the smiles of those who are in on a secret. Apparently they knew I was going to be invited into the group, and if I accepted, that I would be auditioned there and then. Lucky for me I had no idea, or my nerves would have caused yet more havoc than they did.

During my dubious music career, I had found ways of circumventing shyness in order to sing solo; my techniques depended on drugs and alcohol, as well as an assumed persona that I could use as a mask. I had already discovered singing Sri Chinmoy's songs required the stripping away of outer techniques so the true voice of the heart could shine out, or better: its sovereign occupant, the soul. The real self, and not the ego, was therefore necessarily exposed. That frightened me more than anything. As a born perfectionist, and one with a good musical ear, I also knew when I was singing a note technically incorrectly, and could not bear to hear it in such beautiful music. All these factors combined to create an anomaly: one who was capable of singing well, but who simultaneously shackled herself with shyness and unrealistic standards. Although singing by myself at home or in a group provided enough of a shield to give my best, I was simply incapable of singing those songs solo. I thus knew I could do well in *Temple-Song-Hearts* with the company of others, but was sure I would not survive an audition.

I recognised the introduction from the tape, and had the score in front of me, so I knew exactly what to do. It was a rousing and joyous song with magnificent intervals, bursting with expression and life. My rendition was confused, small and timorous; a sparrow with a beak full of treacle would have done a more convincing job. Although the pianist could not have understood my predicament, fortunately as a professional musician she at least had the sense to register it, and the decency to sing along with me. Even that one other voice was enough company for me, and my capacity was meanwhile conspicuous enough for her to appraise it.

As Sri Chinmoy himself had formed the group, I was told his blessings would be sought for my inclusion, so a new photograph would be taken and sent to him. If he accepted me as a member,

I would make the two-hundred-mile round trip to London every Sunday for practices, and I could join any upcoming concerts. My demeanour was seemly and my conversation courteous until it was time to leave, but as I closed the front door behind me, I ran and skipped along that respectable West London street. After a safe distance, I dared let out a whoop of joy.

* * *

Disciples from Britain, and some from Europe, clustered at the arrival hall in Heathrow's Terminal 3. Their greetings buzzed around me, brimming with anticipation of the Master's appearance, but most of them had seen him only weeks before in New York. I had never seen him at all. Aware of this fact, a few kindly made space for me at the front without me asking. I gazed out from the barrier into the strip of empty floor, amidst the canned announcements and artificial light, waiting for my Guru to appear in the world as he had done so many times in my heart.

Somewhere inside the bustle was a bubble of quietude, where for the first time I genuinely sought aloneness. There was the same familiar feeling in the centre of my chest as I had felt before, like the press of many tiny fingers. Inside it that time, I was aware of a flat disc rotating slowly. Tiny parts unfolded from its centre, as if each had always fitted neatly into the other, waiting only for that moment. It was like the intricate workings of some fantastical safe as it unlocked, one layer inside the other inside the other, the colours of each deeper level more vivid than the last. When I was sure the scene in my heart could not be more brilliant or beautiful, the outer doors slid open, and my Guru appeared: neither in the robes of an Asian monk, nor in a satin dhoti, but in a thick down jacket, track pants and running shoes. His head was bare, and a familiar hand peeped out from the end of a padded sleeve. He walked slowly with a full smile, gazing about from one side to another, but seeming to see another realm altogether. Barely six feet away, he looked right into me with eyes made of endless galaxies. Tears swelled in mine, and more tears and more tears again: they would not stop for twelve hours.

Equipped with an unglamorous wad of paper napkins from a restaurant, I took my red velvet seat at the Albert Hall that evening. Had I come for a theatrical performance, I would have been studying a printed programme, or the lighting, or the ornate mouldings. As it was, I had enough to do catching the tears that had been raining steadily all day from just one glimpse of my spiritual Master, and inwardly attempting to prepare myself for several hours in his presence.

I was briefly introduced to a girl sitting behind, but my incapacity for small talk was obvious, and it was not the time for chatting anyway. Although she was about as old as me, a child's pure beauty glowed in her face, as if she had just arrived from some far gentler world. Everything of her seemed fringed in pale gold that brightened when she smiled. To me it was baffling that anyone could reach adulthood and still have so much sweetness to spare.

I was fortunate to have a front corner of the stalls, so I could see only the stage if I looked towards it, as if I comprised the only audience. Sri Chinmoy's instruments had taken their places too: a sculptural array of polished wood and keys and strings. There was an echoed hush gathering momentum in the air, which I tried not to spoil with sniffling. The Master arrived from behind a curtain, a powder blue dhoti gliding about him like ripples of sky. The hush was then complete, as if breath itself had stopped to listen. The opening meditation was a silent overture, making an empty firmament in which new sounds could then take flight. The esraj gave a seamless husky call, one note yearning for the next. A western flute called out its mellow melting warmth, yet still seemed to mirror the surrounding silence. A dance of strings responded brightly to the Master's coaxing. The beauty was not just in the sounds themselves; it was also visibly in Sri Chinmoy's handling, as if his heart and fingers were drawing forth the truest, sweetest and most powerful voice in each.

My Guru reached slowly for a glass of water at his side, and looked up as he brought it toward him. Although he was still much further away than when I had first seen him, it seemed he was looking directly into me in just the same way as earlier that day. The gaze continued unbroken while he drank and replaced the glass. I could have counted the seconds on one hand, but even time seemed drawn into the stillness around him. The notes of the harmonium hung then as backdrops in the air, and he sang. I was only heart: one vast affirmative in that striking yet mellifluous flow of sound.

Deep chimes chanted low and long at the hammer's command. Sri Chinmoy was improvising, but the first few notes were identical to one of the purer pilgrim songs I had kept from my past, played on similar chimes or bells. Rather than coincidence, I chose to take it as another secret symbol of acknowledgement. The finale was a grand piano in the closest corner of the stage – the initial hush then reaching its destination. The Master was so near I could almost have sat beside him, but every space was taken by music anyway: surging, climbing, dancing, building, thundering then glowing, in an immense explosion of spontaneous creativity.

In contest with my joy, I felt something was writhing furiously in both my legs. It was a familiar feeling, only far worse than ever before. I could only grip my seat and will myself not to stand or call out. My own resolve was nothing against that power. In my twisting anguish I wanted to pray, but found I did not know how. I gave out a silent plea anyway, not trusting its potency. A seemingly incongruous memory came winging to me from another age: at once an instant description and instruction. Praying is like my four-year-old self, talking to my grandparents in the tape recorder. It requires faith, patience, self-offering, and complete surrender to God's Will in the form of a result.

Meditation is like hearing a voice on the telephone: there might be slight delays if the line is not perfect, but it is otherwise direct and requires no effort other than listening. I almost forgot the urgency of my plight in the study of that analogy, and Sri Chinmoy was already standing for the final meditation. A tangible peace filtered through me from the newborn silence, as if in answer to my prayer, and we all stood to applaud him.

That night, lying in the cot of a hostel dormitory, I did not want to lose the day in sleep. *Supreme* chanted spontaneously in my heart, so I felt it ringing in my chest and limbs. Behind my closed eyes were only speeding galaxies. I raced through them, weightless as an arrow, letting the tears rain into my hair and pillow.

* * *

I waited by the clean-shaven lawns of Oxford's Christ Church the next evening, wrapped in a sari and cowled shawl. A door of darkened wood separated me from the inside, but I knew not to open it. The seats were in much shorter supply than they had been in London, and so would be given to the public first. Naturally I did not want to deprive anyone of the Master's presence, and after all I had received the day before, I had nothing to complain about, but I dared hope there was a place for me. Nearer the start I was suddenly tense, like a child separated from her parent. I looked to the big wooden door and gave a silent prayer, according to my new technique. As if charmed, the iron latch gave way immediately, and I was ushered in. A few others were allowed to follow, and we could perch on sidelong pews almost behind the stage.

Although many of the instruments were the same, the feeling was entirely different. Instead of rich velvet chairs and cavernous vastness, the wood and whitened stone gave a more traditionally spiritual atmosphere. I could not see more than Sri Chinmoy's feet as he moved about the stage, and the bases of some of the instruments beneath the backdrop, so my inner worlds comprised most of my vision. The difference was in more than the outer situation though; Sri Chinmoy seemed to be playing in a way I had not heard the night before, as if responding to the new environs, giving sympathetically and sensitively according to his inspiration, or perhaps according to what was needed. My overwhelmed tears had run dry, and despite the rigid pews, there was no discomfort. I was transported to the natural joy of a child, smiling then and all the way into my sleep that night.

Back in Heathrow's Terminal 3, as I waited for my Guru's departure, I reflected on the many aspects of him I had witnessed even in the span of days, each as charming and authentic as the next. Who could know how many more were contained in that single form? He looked small and grandfatherly as he entered that day, seating himself on a folding chair between two gaudy shops. A rustling bag of chocolates was placed as prasad on the ground, so near him I almost felt too shy to take one, but he was only soft smiles and affection for everyone. *Can a spiritual Master be cute as well?* I wondered.

I remembered the maple leaves strewn on the ground in childhood, each its own brilliant masterpiece that would never recur and could not be copied. I thought how many times I had eaten chocolate like the little foil-wrapped bar softening in my hand, but the taste was new and notable that day. Seeing the Master on one occasion would be to see only one aspect of him: an aspect and resulting experience that itself may never be repeated. Just as one concert was diametrically different from the following one, the Guru who carried galaxies in his eyes and summoned the power of oceans from only a grand piano, was the same Guru who sat before me right then, with a little zipped travelling bag on his knee, the label of his sports jacket sticking out at the neck by mistake, only adding endearment to an already endearing image.

It was then, clasping an empty sweet-wrapper, in an especially dingy section of cheerless Heathrow, that I knew for certain this Guru and this spiritual family would be enough for me. I was more grateful in that moment than any time I could remember: grateful I had trusted the instinct to make space in my heart, without knowing how or when it would be filled; grateful I had not settled at the base camps of empty pleasures or hollow promises or shallow victories, but had continued climbing alone until I found the guide who would usher me higher. True, I was only packing my bags and lacing my boots for the ascent, and the peak would no doubt be muffled in mist for this lifetime and many more, but I knew there would be more joy than I had ever known just in the climb itself. I remembered the words of Lao-Tsu, as I had heard a decade before: 'a journey of a thousand miles begins with a single step.'

11

Fire and Dragons

Unless and until you extinguish
The fire of wild separativity,
You will never be granted
The moon-white feeling
Of oneness-love. [11]
—Sri Chinmoy

After seeing my Guru for the first time, landing back in daily life gave quite a jolt. As a spiritual seeker in a mostly secular world, I would need to grow used to such transitions. Although I was still busy easing into my new routines, it was already clear I could better maintain them amongst people with similar priorities. The switch from my interior world to the outer would be less stark and disorienting if the distance between them was shorter. Alison liked to talk incessantly, watch television at a grating volume, drink wine until the early hours, and invite her boyfriend to stay at weekends – all of which were normal choices for someone leading a more worldly life than the one I had chosen. Although she liked to rib me about my comparatively insular nature, I knew that was also just her way, and it was not appropriate for me to wish she was otherwise. The decision was mutual and amicable: we would both seek new company.

My desk phone rang in a strange way a few days later: the rare tone of an outside call. It was Alison at home, hyperventilating and leapfrogging from one panic attack to another. I knew she struggled daily with stress, and masked it with talking and television, in the same way as I used to patch my own unhappiness with drugs and alcohol. I had no idea what to do for someone in her state, but the phone was her lifeline, and there was only me at the end of it. I began talking through the most basic breathing exercises I had learned in classes, not knowing if they would work for someone so desperate. Eventually she could speak coherently, so I assured her I would be there as soon as possible. She was curled in a whimpering ball on her bed when I got home: the same position I had been in ten years earlier.

'I'm sorry,' she snuffled, half to her pillow and half to me.

'Don't be, I'm glad you called.'

'I mean sorry for making fun of you. I know I have to learn to relax but I'm too scared and it's too difficult and you know how to do it and I've got to learn. Will you teach me?'

'Yes, later. Right now you need a hot bath and a cup of tea.'

After I had let her sob out the details of the latest fight with her boyfriend and the nasty things her boss had said to her at work, I set up a little candle and talked through a concentration exercise.

'I can't do it,' she said after less than a minute.

'You can't do it *yet* you mean. You can with practice.'

'Is that all I need to know? How can that possibly help? It's not going to work.'

'It's not about knowing, it's about trying: every day, whether you feel like it or not, whether you think you can do it or not. It's not necessarily easy, but it's definitely simple. Anyone can do it if they really want to, and you *do* really want to, so you *can*. Just try for another minute.'

A minute later she was already keeling with drowsiness, and slept like a kitten then for twelve hours, which was probably for the best. Although she pretended much too chirpily that nothing had happened in the morning, she later showed me the back pages of her diary where my suggestions were carefully written out, like bullet points from a business presentation. I knew her well enough to take that as thanks. Although talkative, ironically she was never much of a communicator.

The same week I had a call from a colleague in the legal department, to request a private meeting. She was known as the Welsh Dragon. Her words were like pips of fire that she spat out into the world. She swooped through the offices arbitrarily, casting a great gloomy shadow beneath her. Of the four developers in my department, I had been chosen for the punishing task of serving her, because of my apparently mild temperament.

'The meek shall inherit the earth,' my boss would say as I left for my Dragon meetings: more mockingly than prophetically, but still by way of an oblique compliment. So far, it seemed I had only inherited trouble.

My colleagues regarded me much as my family had done while I was growing up: a benign enigma, a creature of some likeable, harmless, but otherwise undocumented species. While my co-workers went to the pub at lunchtime, I was in my car learning songs or meditating. While they kept pictures of their pets and offspring on their desks, I just had a vase of fresh flowers and a portrait of a man who was obviously neither spouse nor blood relation. Most people did not comment on the picture at all, if they even noticed. The ones who asked anything probably did so out of politeness anyway, rather than any real interest, but the Welsh Dragon's interrogations came frequently and without mercy. I kept my answers brief and direct, knowing any response would meet with a sneer of cynicism.

Private meetings were almost unheard of. It was a young, forward-looking company where everyone went by the first name. Almost all the meeting areas were open plan, so it was an effort to even book somewhere with a door, and a good walk to get there. I assumed such places were only kept for firing people, or at least lambasting them for a serious offence. I could not imagine what crime I had committed, but I was sure only my doom lurked inside that windowless room.

Although the Dragon was already there, I barely recognised

her: she was smiling. There was no mention of work at all; a friend of hers was sinking fast in a mire of depression, and no words of encouragement seemed to help. She wanted to know what Sri Chinmoy would recommend for such a person, as she knew he was a 'wise man'. My mind was sprinting to catch up, but she was already peering expectantly into my face. I wrenched my thoughts together, and first reeled off a string of caveats: mainly that I was an absolute beginner in spirituality, and that her friend would be well advised to seek medical help straight away. Not entirely sure what would come out of my mouth next, I remembered a passage I had read that week which related perfectly to the subject, and amply answered her question. I then described a few techniques her friend might try, to help her to relax once she was through the worst, just as I had done with Alison.

With a kindness that was definitely rare and presumably costly for her, the Dragon put her hand on mine as she thanked me. Since we still had the room for a while longer she confided secrets from her own life that would have left the soft underbelly of her character exposed if she thought I was prone to gossip. My legs could barely carry me back to my desk when it was over, so I first wandered bewildered around the grounds. Being different was nothing new: at home, at school, and finally at work. Although I had learned to accept it by then, for the first time I started to wonder if it could be a strength rather than a handicap. I had always assumed being unusual meant I was wrong, but maybe that perception itself was the only thing out of place. It would take a few years longer for that idea to grow in certainty.

* * *

I had managed to knock a big enough dent in my debts to apply for a mortgage on a flat, but the ones in my price range put me off altogether. They were either crumbling tumbledown places that would cost more to make safe than they would to buy, or they were small sterile crate-like places on a new estate near work, that looked like they might blow over in a storm. My hope glowed anew when I learned the café would need a place for one of its workers, so if I took a larger flat nearer town, I could rent out a room, and thus cover the higher mortgage. Although much more down-to-earth than well-to-do Clifton, most of Montpelier, with its garden allotments and farm shops and homespun artisans, was still outside my dreams. There was a single possibility: a quirky place behind Montpelier Station, part of a converted warehouse. The owner wanted a quick sale, but the agent had nothing similar to value it against, so had priced it cautiously low – in fact within a whisker of my budget. Five minutes walk in one direction was the café, and five minutes the other way was the Meditation Centre in Bishopston. Providence seemed to have everything in hand.

It was the only place I looked at inside, but even from the doorstep I was besotted. At the back was a new white bathroom tiled in sapphire blue. It had a domed window in the ceiling that looked straight up into the sky, so one could see the stars from the bathtub. There was one large bedroom with a similar window, and a smaller one with a long slanted skylight showering everything in sun. The front was like part of a handsome coach house, overlooking a cobbled alley. There was a white kitchen and a wide lounge with twin mullioned windows, whose sills were deep enough for sitting on or for growing things in pots. Above was a hipped roof, making a loft for storage. Underneath, in a shared place made of concrete, there was even space for my car to live. I bought it for forty thousand pounds, with only two thousand to offer in deposit. Soon after that, house prices skyrocketed, so I was one of the last to grasp the property ladder's lowest rung with so little capital and so modest an income.

Before my new flatmate moved in, the carpet was thrown

away, and I had fresh wood flooring laid throughout. I took a week off to whitewash every room, and to equip each with new white and blue furniture. Apart from some potted herbs, cut flowers, and a few carefully chosen pictures, the rest of the space was left deliberately clear. The result was simple and homely, yet immaculate.

When it was done, and I lay down to let the stars gaze on me through the dome of my room, my first thoughts were only grateful. I then realised I had been alone almost all week without noticing. The strange sinister presence that had pressed on me for twenty-seven years had moved out of my life, and with it the nightmares. For the first time ever, I could not remember what it was like to be afraid just because I was by myself. It was the same robust purity and invincible safety that I had only felt at my grandparents' house in childhood. Things I thought I would have to lug around on my back forever seemed to be falling away, without any effort on my part.

Meanwhile one thing I thought was gone had begun sneaking back again. Just as on my return from Thailand, I would become physically drained for no apparent reason. My body was like some device whose batteries needed replacing – there was no point coaxing or chivvying it, as there was nothing left worth chivvying. The dense fog of fatigue would descend and lift seemingly of its own volition. I could be walking along quite capably one moment, then the road ahead would suddenly grow insurmountable, and I would have to sit on somebody's garden wall. I thought meditation had taken away that blight forever, but it seemed instead I had only been granted a brief reprieve. Without knowing the cause of the challenge, at least I still had faith that my life was in God's Hands, and I assumed it was something I had to bear. I did not tell anyone about it then – I would not even admit it to myself at first. At that stage though, even a bad day could be glossed over, so I just got on with it.

Boys in the Centre often socialised separately from the girls.

As I had always been more used to male company, that took some adjustment, but my place soon became a popular female haunt, and was fondly nicknamed *The Ashram*. A few of us would often meet there on Saturdays for dinner and a movie, or during the week for extra singing. After a few short-term tenants, one girl from the café moved in to the spare room more permanently.

It became like a second home for the Spanish girl. She lived close by in Redland, but was finding it difficult to reconcile her spiritual life with a house full of students. I recognised all too well her dragging feet and extended conversations at the end of an evening, knowing her housemates would be drunk or listening to loud music at home, and that her spiritual nourishment would drain away from her before she even got to bed. My mortgage was turning out to be more of a strain than I hoped, mostly because I was still paying interest on a whole smorgasbord of loans from London. As her parents were quite well off, she was used to more space than most people, so I offered to rent her my room, and I would section off part of the living room for myself. It suited everybody perfectly.

Someone was shouting *FIRE!* one night, and the three of us were on the street in our pyjamas before we knew any more than that. The owners of an Italian restaurant across the alley had called the fire brigade, and were standing in their doorway to meet us. The warehouse separating our flat from a wholesale supermarket was coughing out thick smoke. Yellow flames had devoured a stack of folded boxes at the front, and were licking hungrily towards barrels of cooking oil under an awning. Inside was already a furnace, the roof and struts collapsing like matchwood.

'Come and wait upstairs,' blustered the Italian man, offering me his own slippers for my bare feet before digging out more for the other two and heaping blankets on our shoulders. Our neighbour downstairs was away on holiday, and the other two flats had evacuated onto the back road, so we allowed ourselves to be bustled upwards, watching then and praying from the restaurant balcony.

The fire engine came quickly and snuffed out the worst of it, at least before it reached the oil stacked up in front like a cache of explosives. Although smoke had gone in through our open kitchen window, there was nothing more serious from what we could see. The firemen were chatting and reeling away their hoses, while we cheered with relief. The Italian man only grew more animated though, shouting down and pointing up at the same time. Against the black night it was barely visible even from our raised vantage, but if I squinted I could see a thin grey plume drifting out of our roof, another seeping out from the side, and a faint flicker like a reflection in the sky. A series of wooden beams had connected the warehouse to our building for support. One had burned away completely, but the blazing stump of it had tunnelled through the wall of our smallest bedroom, growing fatter by the second on the feast of our interior. It took another half hour to quell the new fire and to check it had not spread further. By then our home was little more than a bombsite.

As the owner, only I was allowed back in, and then only briefly under supervision until the structure had been checked more thoroughly. All that had been pure white just hours before was blackened, or grey with soot at best. I collected my keys, money, phone, a Transcendental Picture, and a smoky change of clothes for two of us. The smallest bedroom could have passed as a coal pit. A pale dawn sky peered through the yawning roof, and by that light I could see only shreds of plaster and unrecognisable fragments of belongings: sodden scraps of books, stumps of wood, black rags.

The other flats were deemed safe, so after offering us tea and consolation, the neighbours were back in their homes as usual. When the firemen had left, the Red Cross waited for us outside. They gave us a packaged jogging suit for the girl still in her pyjamas, and some welcome kindness. As nobody was hurt, there was nothing more they could do. I opened the doors of the garage to find my little white hatchback smiling out at me. It was warmer inside than usual, but the concrete walls had at least kept out the flames. We had transport, and we had one another. It was a good start.

Huddled at a little round table in the café, we three had a joint revelation: individually each one of us might have been shattered by the blow, but together we made one perfect invincible being in three parts. One was patient and pragmatic, steadfast as a rock in the turbulent oceans of life; one was efficient and fast, with a logical mind and a gift for problem solving; one floated above all setbacks with her warm cheerfulness and affection. We would need each person's strengths equally, at least to get us through that first day.

Once she had tearfully salvaged a few items, the girl whose room was rubble moved out somewhere else for a while, and the other went straight into university exams. I knew the contents of the flat were insured, and I had paid buildings insurance to the management company, so it should be just a sequence of stepping stones to get everything back the way it was.

In fact the building was not covered at all: the management company had taken our money, but kept it for themselves instead of buying a policy. I called round a builder I knew I could trust, to see how much the repairs would be. He guessed at twenty thousand pounds. Adding insult to injury, I heard from a neighbour that the fire had been an arson attack. The warehouse had been due for demolition the following day; by first setting light to it themselves, the supermarket owners could claim the 'accidental' loss on their insurance, and still go ahead with the demolition as planned. A camera in the alley had picked up a man starting the fire, but the image was too blurry to show who it was. In theory he could have been just a passing pyromaniac, but we were all sure it was a scam.

My sunny resolve dissolved completely. Why did I have to

share the planet with such rogues? Some innocent person could have been hurt or even killed, while the guilty ones lined their own pockets. I slumped in my grey kitchen on a grimy chair and sobbed for an hour. I genuinely resented being single then. Although my housemates had lost many more treasured belongings than I had, at least they were not legally bound to the tattered fabric of the house as I was, and nobody was bound to me. I felt very much alone in my sad sooty little world.

I did not ask for rescue, but it came in droves. The Centre Leader took all our remaining clothes away to wash the smoke out of them. News spread further afield too: people from Centres around the country sent gifts of money and clothes and books for the girl who had lost everything. The Bristol boys came round with shovels, facemasks and their oldest overalls to clear the wreckage from the small room. They looked like a rum bunch of trainee miners afterwards, and were just as jolly at the end as when they had started. The builder lent a tarpaulin to keep out the rain, and had one of his lads tie it in place on the roof. A short-term extension was arranged on the mortgage with mysterious ease, and I got a sudden raise at work that neatly covered the extra repayments, as well as the loss of rent. My family came at the weekend, along with every member of Bristol Centre, to start cleaning and repainting.

I stood in the middle of it all at one point, and noticed there was barely any space for me in my own home; every surface and corner was a hive of happy scraping and scrubbing, sloshing and sanding. *How could I have thought I was alone?* I wondered. *How could I wish to exchange all this for marriage? One extra person could never be enough.* Until that moment I had assumed being single meant being self-sufficient; really it meant being God-sufficient. True, I was taking outer help from others in that charred mess, and very gladly, but I had let God send whomever He chose, instead of expecting a specific person to behave in a particular way. Emotionally I could thus remain free, and so could those around me. Admittedly it was difficult to let go and trust Him in practice, especially during an emergency, but I treasured the lesson much more for seeing it first hand: with paint and buckets and scouring pads for proof. It seemed with my wayward nature that perhaps I would only discover the depth of my faith via disasters like fires and car crashes anyway. By having to lean on God through others, I also began a long lesson in humility. For one who had always been fiercely independent rather than God-dependent, that lesson would not come cheaply.

I realised then how strong a foundation even my newborn inner life had laid for me. Although it was there every day, its soundness was more apparent in a storm. I did not weather that particular calamity easily, but neither did I fall apart in it. My own daily meditation practice and twice-weekly visits to the Centre were each like tiny bricks that fit together in a growing fortress, to shield me from life's buffets and the full force of its blows. Little did I know how I would need that mounting strength in future times.

My home was given and destroyed and rebuilt again, perhaps all by the same hand of fate. I would get back almost all the cost of the repairs in two years with the help of a good barrister. The outer balance would thus be restored in time, and I would be back where I started. Inwardly though, I was much better off than I had been. It was easier to see life as God's Game, where the scammers and scoundrels, family and firemen, lawyers and loyal friends had each pitched me the ball of opportunity, whether or not that had been their intention.

* * *

A girl stretched out her lungs and heart as one with eight others, the single note in nine twined parts launching from the rise of a piano to soar across a sea of smiles. Her loosely tethered hair fell in dark waves against the pastel glow of an Indian sari. There was no thought except that one note's offering, and the Bengali phrase to come: Ekla ami chalbona ar – I shall no longer walk alone. Just those words could bring a flood to her exultant green-blue eyes. An ocean of thankfulness rose in her chest, but she knew she must not let it spill, only stretch and stretch to contain it, remaining still and standing. On the front row of the audience, an Indian man in a blue wool coat and brimming silence traversed his own inner worlds of meditation.

In Cardiff City Hall that autumn, I knew a little better who I was than when I had last looked out from a stage. Having never felt so much at once, I only hoped I was not dreaming. Sri Chinmoy had returned to Britain for the second time in a year, to offer two concerts. The first was in Cardiff, dedicated to Diana Princess of Wales, who had passed away just weeks before, and whom the Master had met in London the day he had played at the Royal Albert Hall. The second was in Cambridge, in honour of Sri Chinmoy's own Guru – Sri Aurobindo – who had studied at King's College. My auspicious debut with *Temple-Song-Hearts* formed a prelude to the concert in Wales.

I had spent most of the day and the night before in somebody's living room with my artist friend. We had volunteered to make a Welsh dragon as a backdrop. It needed to be twenty feet long, conjured only from the rolls of chicken wire and golden gift-wrap stacked up in the hallway. Neither of us had attempted anything on that scale before, so we were probably not sufficiently daunted. We had a tape measure, wire cutters, scissors, pencil and paper – how difficult could it be?

There was not space to lay it all out in one piece and still have room for industry, so from a paper grid we sketched out strange dismembered pieces, to be assembled at the hall. We worked as one harmonious mind and body with four connected arms. Time seemed to accelerate towards the dawn though, and despite having not had a moment's rest, the final claw was only attached to its huge drumstick leg as the van pulled in to collect us. We pinched it all together with wire and pliers by the stage, and gave it to the boys to hang with fishing line. Perhaps in our relief or tiredness we did not impress on them sufficiently the importance of supporting the tongue.

A Welsh dragon is not a Welsh dragon without its spear-like tongue. We had made ours red in extravagant contrast to the body. As Sri Chinmoy sat down at the harmonium that evening, the dragon's tongue also swivelled down toward the open lid of the piano, and we two creators prayed in horror. There was no telling for sure where it would fall or when, but it could certainly hurt the Master if he did not see it coming. Just before he took his seat at the piano the tongue peeled away and shot straight down behind the stage, missing both Guru and instrument. The once mighty dragon looked like an innocuous winged puppy without it. Despite our chagrin, we were both just glad the worst was over.

The sting of our remorse was short-lived. 'I praise you,' Sri Chinmoy had issued as our performance had drawn to a close. Apparently he said later all nine of us were like goddesses when we sang that night. They were the first compliments I had received from him, and although I did not dare take the latter literally, for fear it would go to my head, I treasured it no less than if it were an established fact.

* * *

Once I knew the *Temple-Song-Hearts* repertoire and a few popular songs that we sang on Centre nights, I decided to memorise the Master's longest song to date: *Dyulok Chariye*. It was a poem he had written for Sri Aurobindo at the age of fifteen. The two hundred and twelve lines had been set to music only two years previously. I practised it on my morning run and on the way to work, I woke up with it turning in my head like a dawn mantra, and it whispered me asleep at night like a lullaby. Immersing myself in that song, I developed a far deeper affinity with my Guru's music than I had through only hearing it, almost as if I dared then consider myself a member of its family. Although I knew Sri Chinmoy's songs had all been written in devotion to God, I also realised they were written for those of us still climbing to the peaks of our own perfection: emboldening and strengthening us like the ancient songs of pilgrimage. They spoke to me of my own striving, at once reminding me why and how to continue. It took two months before I could complete that one song without the score. No song would ever seem daunting after that, so I went about collecting more of them in my memory, each one with its own unique offering and personality. The adventure was its own reward.

Bengali words were a mystery to me, but somehow I preferred learning Sri Chinmoy's songs written in his native language to those in my own. The challenge of learning itself seemed to clear the mind for meditation, in the same way as running did. Even from my first meditation class, I found its transforming magic did not depend on my mental comprehension anyway – the music spoke directly to my heart. Sometimes I would read translations, or pick out a few key words; often I preferred just to sense the meanings of the songs. Silence still daunted and puzzled me most of the time, and singing seemed to bring me as much inner nourishment as quiet meditation anyway – sometimes more.

According to Sri Chinmoy, and as I had already experienced for myself, paramount amongst the qualities needed for singing spiritual songs is soulfulness. A rare reminder came to me sometimes while singing: a lucid fragrance that I knew was not in the room. Jasmine or lily or rose, it was always something recognisable, pure and fresh, but not from any outer source. I could not make it come at will; it was a gift that arrived spontaneously, as if from soulfulness itself. When singing alone, however technical perfection tempted me, I thus knew with more certainty not to seek it at the expense of the soul's true voice.

Technical correctness is particularly desirable when singing in a group, especially while performing for the public. I therefore struggled harder not to let perfection dethrone soulfulness during concerts. Other situations would present themselves in public too, so just the mechanics of standing still and singing kept me on my toes, let alone maintaining a meditative consciousness. Luckily one of the primary profits of meditation is an increase in poise: a quality Sri Chinmoy valued highly, and which shone through his every action.

I spent one performance literally on the tips of my toes, as the stage had been rearranged since the sound check. My assigned position left me teetering on the brink of a recess full of plants, praying I would not disappear down the long leafy shaft that gaped behind me like a trap in a jungle floor. A fly shot straight into one girl's ear at the start of another concert, and buzzed there for the rest of the first half. When we would have been meditating in the interval, we were instead trying to funnel in sparkling water – the only sort in the dressing room – to drown out the occupant. To remain poised when one knows a cockroach is climbing up the outside of one's sari, or a raging tickle is clawing up the inside of one's throat, requires more a samurai's steel than the female seemliness apparent to the audience. Once honed though, that inner strength can translate to any life circumstance.

Singing with *Temple-Song-Hearts* was outwardly an honour: a chance to offer the same music to the world that had spoken to my own heart in classes. Inwardly it was to spin three plates at once: soulfulness, perfection and – most elusive of all to me – confidence. During our Sunday practices, I came to believe one could potentially learn all spiritual lessons just by singing Sri Chinmoy's songs in a group. This was further confirmed later when I heard the Master suggested not three, but eight qualities for singers to focus on: consciousness, oneness, sweetness, soulfulness, confidence, perfection, cheerfulness and gratitude. To grasp and maintain all those virtues simultaneously while singing would certainly be more than a lifetime's work in itself for me, but it was easily worth the endeavour. I knew their mastery would depend on my daily sincerity, and not just a fleeting inner pep talk before a performance.

In order to face the gaping void where my confidence should have been, I studied Sri Chinmoy's teachings on shyness. I sulked after the first reading, but only because I knew from many years of hiding behind the coattails of the world that his words were true, at least for me. Shyness is not a sweet or mild quality after all, but one harboured by those who secretly *want* attention, rather than those who seek to avoid it. Shyness is thus not equivalent to modesty or humility. Humility means living naturally according to one's higher nature, neither needing acclaim nor heeding denigration; shyness wears the same self-consciousness as pride, only it is more subtle, and therefore harder to catch. Little did I know even that seemingly meek weakness was a force to be reckoned with. Rather than confronting it, Sri Chinmoy taught instead to develop its antidote: oneness, the conscious awareness of unity with God and all His creation.

To feel oneness with my singing companions, who had become like sisters to me, was no effort at all, but standing in public without a veil for my personality was another matter. To master that fear with integrity, I would need to sing increasingly to the real selves in the audience from my own real self, from my soul to theirs, from the God in me to the God in them. Thus there would be only one familiar Person in the audience, rather than a mass of teeming strangers, each with two expectant eyes on me.

These outer challenges were somewhat eased by a new inner friendship with music. Since first hearing Sri Chinmoy's own performances – in person or on recordings – I would often imagine the instrument as part of my own heart. When a string was plucked or bowed, I would feel the same sweet ache as I had noticed first in classes, the sound's vibration radiating as if from my own chest. Sometimes a similar sensation would come without any outer melody at all, but only inner sound: during meditation, or even while walking and going about my daily chores. It only happened when I was happy. If ever it went away for a day or two, I usually realised I needed to attend my inner weather; it was thus a useful barometer of consciousness.

The inner music was something apart from the banal cogwheels of my mind, which left to their own devices would summon no more than a supermarket jingle, or a flaccid tune from the radio. Perhaps it was imagination, even though it seemed too real and beautiful to be something of my own creation. A few times I tried to control it mentally to see what would happen, but it would just carry on in its own way for a while, then gently recede and vanish. I decided not to question where it came from then; just to welcome it and let it enchant me.

Sometimes it was one instrument, improvising in a way that could not have been captured or transcribed, even if I had wanted to try; sometimes it was a voice like my own, following a melody that wandered through the forests of eternity without words or breath or beginning; sometimes it was many harmonious voices in weaving echoing refrains; other times it was only a panoply of rich percussive rhythms in many complex parts, or the lively caper of a single drum. Later there were instruments that I had never heard on earth, but their sounds would need more space and silence than the world could afford anyway. I dreamed of them one night, suspended in the sky as big as buildings and as far apart as cities, playing an impossible symphony into the quietude. The world seemed cramped and heavy in comparison when I awoke again.

12

New York

You want to go out
And see the world.
God wants you to come home
And become the world. [12]
—Sri Chinmoy

I was never any good at ice-skating. By the time I had mustered the courage and mobility to let go the buffered edges of the rink, my hands were numb with cold, my ankles had swollen from levering me upright, my trousers were soaked from falling over, and it was already time to go home. Meanwhile others turned tight pirouettes in the glittering centre, or whistled past me, weaving backwards on nothing but two slippery blades. So it felt on my first visit to New York for April Celebrations, only in that case I persevered beyond my initial ungainliness.

There seemed to be three Gurus in one, and I had not yet tried to reconcile them. That balancing act was at the root of my challenge. The first aspect was the Guru I meditated on every day in the Transcendental Picture: ageless, nameless, beyond all human need and artifice, at once a silent staff for my worldly traverse, and a porthole on the rolling Universe beyond.

The second was the Guru in my dreams: inwardly all these, but outwardly personal and approachable, like a grandparent. In my nightly inner wanderings I would sometimes find myself in the back seat of his car, or in his house, or in a public place: either alone or with others, and always without any barrier to speech. I could run to him and give him things, or ask him questions whenever I liked. He wore polo shirts, shorts and running shoes; he joked and chatted, or sometimes gently reprimanded if I made a mistake, always with fathomless deeps of concern and wisdom where there would be eyes.

The third was my outer Guru: both these former aspects combined, and more besides, yet he lived beyond a sheer screen of etiquette, where I could see him but not seek his company. Although I had already seen him outwardly in England, and had ample confirmation from him that I belonged in his presence, I had not prepared myself for being just one of many hundreds of disciples who also called him 'Guru,' who also meditated on their own Transcendental Pictures, and who probably had sweet personal experiences with him in their dreams as well. My main obstacle was discovering that those who had known him for many years also had sweet personal experiences with him *outwardly*. It was simply not practical for him to give his overt attention to all and sundry – exclusion was certainly not in his nature, as I knew from my inner world. I was a new disciple so I was expected to remain some distance from him, as just one tiny drop in an ocean of spiritual aspirants. That was more of a challenge than I had imagined, but the growth it fostered would bear unimaginable fruits in time.

It was not the New York I had seen in films: all yellow taxis and brownstone buildings, swarming crosswalks full of super-models and Wall Street traders. If I had harboured any doubt that my Guru had left his Indian ashram life to be of spiritual service to the West, rather than just chasing the opulence of America for his own ends, that doubt would not have survived in the area where he made his home. Jamaica, Queens: neon nail bars and used car dealerships, 99¢ stores and discount shoes in mesh buckets by the road, where howling sirens compete with Latin beats until the sacred hours of the night. It may not have been a traditional choice for one dedicating his life to inner peace, but it was certainly not the choice of a materialist either.

Somewhere in a patch of detached houses – large by British standards, but simple and mostly a little dour – each morning I left my sleeping bag on my allotted square of floor and wrapped up against the April air for a jog. Breakfast was served al fresco at the edge of Goose Pond Park, on polystyrene plates with plastic forks, as were all our meals. Whatever the weather, it seemed there was always someone up and about earlier than me: cooking or running or practising performances.

On the corner of 164th Street and Normal Road was Aspiration-Ground: previously a tram station, but by then a tennis court, attended by trees and a high fence wound with creeping wisteria vines. Two interior sides were terraced with wooden bleachers. I waited there later in the day, with around a thousand others, for the Master's arrival.

Sri Chinmoy's tennis days were almost at their end. Seated in a simple wood-framed gazebo with two wide doors at the front, he would meditate and sing and exercise and tell stories through a microphone, well into the afternoon. However early I sought a place from which to see him clearly, it seemed others had got there much sooner. Usually prasad and walking meditations on the tennis court itself were my only opportunities to glimpse him properly.

Most of the girls in *Temple-Song-Hearts* had been disciples from an early age: either joining a Centre as children with their families, or alone in their teens. Sri Chinmoy was especially kind and grandfatherly to children. Many years before my arrival, several young girls would sing for him while he meditated or practised his weightlifting. The group was known as Paree's Group, after its leader. Even as they had grown older – most of them by then in their twenties – the girls who had been with him as children would receive the same attention from the Master as they had in their earlier youth. He knew them all personally and spoke to them frequently, often handing them their own special prasad, before the main prasad was laid out in crates some distance from his little hut.

At first I sulked when I saw the friends whom I thought of as sisters, speaking with my Guru as I did in my dreams. Seeing that his smiles and spiritual instruction were for them and not me, I blazed with sadness and jealousy. I was as if back in the doldrums of childhood: alone in the playground while the other children absorbed themselves in games only they understood; alone in the sick bay at camp while everyone else rode horses and shot arrows and swam in the lake. Although surrounded by hundreds of people, and in the presence of my Guru, I rendered myself alone.

I was spoiled with attention from other disciples, and having heard I could sing, they invited me to join a dozen different performances. The evening meetings took place at a public school: PS86 on Parsons Boulevard. Sri Chinmoy would sit at the front, facing the stage in an armchair to observe the presentations, sometimes taking the microphone from beside his seat to offer anecdotes, songs or poems. Large gatherings such as these were known as 'functions', even if they had no set programme. Although I still rarely saw the Master unless I was on stage, a function provided several hours of musical and theatrical acts, which helped to stem my brooding.

On one morning jog, Normal Road seemed anything but normal. Cherry blossom hung in frothy bunches from the grey stalks of trees. Blushing white magnolia blooms, fatter than any I had seen, stretched upwards like hands in prayer. The sky could not have been a cleaner blue, or the sun's fingers any softer. I had cried a good deal that week, and asked myself if I would rather be at home. I knew I was already at home though: more so than anywhere in the world. In that sparkling dawn of spring, I remembered I had chosen the shortest route up the mountain. I would rather not go back to a more comfortable way if that way would be longer, or worse still would lead to a dead end. I felt like a grub, inching along while others could fly, but at least I was in some sort of motion.

I passed a workman making an early start on a decorating job. The pavement was strewn with multicoloured dust and curls of old paint: layers and layers of grime and clashing hues. In places the wood was bare, ready then for a final sanding and a fresh coat of colour. I certainly wanted my old inner paint stripped away too, rather than putting a new coat over dirt and last year's choices. It might be messy for a while, and draughty with my bare wood exposed, but as I already knew from my singing adventures, to learn new ways sometimes meant unlearning old ones first. Just as I had done with music, I would endeavour to forego the flaky veneer of the ego for the sound weatherproofing of the heart.

* * *

Despite my clumsy start, I returned to New York at least for official Celebrations twice a year. By August I knew the inner Guru was still abundantly present, however much or little I glimpsed him outwardly. Just to be in his environs was nourishment in itself, and to see him was more a luxury than a necessity. I watched Paree's Group bared to the relentless sun in peaked hats, while most of us sat under the shelter of trees, and began to accept that they were something apart from me; they surely represented a higher spiritual standard. Not that age was the only prerequisite for inclusion, or a gauge of anything particular, but if nothing else they had the inner merit to find their Guru much earlier in life than I had. Perhaps discovering him at such an age I would not have treasured his presence in my life as dearly as I did by then, not knowing the deceptions and disappointments of the secular world first hand, and not knowing how vulnerable I would be in its storms without the refuge of my spiritual life. I resolved anew to tread my own path, and not to hanker after anyone else's. There was no point wishing

I were any way other than the way God made me.

I remembered the night on the metal bridge, and how I had begged God to let me come home. At the time I assumed that would mean ending the life He had given me, but in fact my stay on earth had barely begun. Of all the unlikely places, I had found home in Jamaica, Queens. The earthly habitat was irrelevant: home was in my heart and in my Guru's presence, uplifted by his love of God and all the service to the world that engendered. I was ashamed of my jealousy then; it showed me I had not kept my side of the bargain. I would take up a tiny corner and quietly absorb myself in any occupation, wishing nothing more from God than to let me grow nearer to Him, all the while learning from my Guru's devoted example.

I realised everything had changed since April, and so radically that it was obvious only I could have changed, while all except the weather stayed as it had been. The sun was a fierce clarion instead of a downy whisper; rivulets of sweat had replaced the goose bumps under my sari. Cicadas creaked and rattled in the trees, and the air felt like steam. In the same way as I sought more oneness with the world through singing, I declared myself a part of my wider spiritual community by serving – I wondered what I might give instead of counting all the things I was not receiving. The more I sang and the more I ran, the more sense life made. I knew it also made more sense when I immersed myself in selfless action rather than just wallowing in my thoughts.

From then I stayed in the driveway if help was needed preparing prasad, even if it meant missing something inside Aspiration-Ground; I volunteered for extra cooking and cleaning shifts, or chose the least desirable ones; I ran in the shorter races and counted laps at the long ones; I picked up litter that was not mine, instead of walking past it with a blind eye; I went out of my way to thank people, and offered gifts of smiles to those who were not yet my friends. In many ways that community seemed a microcosm of some more perfect world than the one I had always known. Although generally a delight to be around, disciples had not reached perfection – they had crabby or downcast or inconsiderate days, just like me – but like me they were also stretching nearer the divine ideal, even in inches. Many were undoubtedly much further ahead than me, but we were all moving towards the same goal. I thus tried to see the divine in all of them and in myself, the way Sri Chinmoy did, even if it was sometimes not so apparent.

I had not become an angel overnight, but focusing more on the outflow rather than the inflow of love changed my world immediately, and I was already far happier than ever before. There were always challenges to my resolve though – for example when the Master invited new girls to join Paree's Group. I studied them from a distance, trying to discern how they differed from me. They were a little younger in age, and had been disciples a little longer than me, so I could have seen it as fair, but the new attention my Guru showered on them still pinched at me. In the next moment I would see the high standards he drew from them – in their soulfulness and their knowledge of songs, in their general propriety and oneness with one another – and knew I was simply not of their calibre.

It would take four years from my first visit to New York before I was truly at peace seeing others nearer my Guru than I could be myself. It was a chance conversation, with someone I hardly knew, on a seemingly unrelated topic, that helped me remember, and sowed the seed of that calm in my heart.

'The Guru gives only what is needed, not what is deserved. Our opportunities cannot be deserved anyway; they all come through God's Grace. The Guru's role is to offer whatever instruction and experience each person needs for their swiftest passage to God.'

Ambling then down Normal Road, and peeping over the fences on my way, I remembered Sri Chinmoy's frequent comparison between the spiritual life and a garden. I realised anew how like a flower each person is. We are all individuals, but each of us forms an intrinsic part of a rich and varied creation, whose abundance and beauty depends on that very variety. Plants all need different environs, and different types of care at various times of year to encourage them to flourish and to reach their absolute potential. A true spiritual Master is like an accomplished gardener, knowing by communion with God precisely the required action and the most appropriate time to deliver it. If the seeker is also ready, then abundant blossoming is sure to follow. Some need fertile soil, frequent watering and special feeding; others grow better in arid ground, where they have to burrow down their roots to become strong. Some need pruning back to their bare bones, while others need freedom to grow. Desert flowers need the sort of sun that would scorch the shady woodland types. Some flower constantly, while others maybe only once in a lifetime. Some are grand and gorgeous, others charming in their simplicity. If they were all treated the same way, only certain ones would thrive, and the richness of creation would be stifled. Is the daisy envious of the rose? Does the daffodil cower in shame before the iris? No, it is far too busy being a daffodil. No matter its shape or size or disposition though, each one strives to grow towards the same epitome of light.

* * *

I was soon to face a challenge that would set me much further apart from others. It would lead me to question my sense of worth yet more deeply, and leave me yet more grateful for my new insight into individual experience. It began that very autumn with a strange virus that spread to almost everyone I knew. Those who were initially fit sprang back again after a couple of weeks, but my strength was already patchy before I caught it, and that further weakness only stayed with me. Any form of exercise was unthinkable then, and often things I had taken for granted – like shopping, or cleaning, or going to work – would turn into complex ordeals.

Apart from filling up my spiral-bound notebook with it all, I only told the doctor at first. She did some tests, but just as when I got back from Thailand, nothing was found. It was thus assumed I was trying to get out of work. Whatever I said to the contrary, the doctor had in her head that I was shirking. If only she knew me – how I abhorred inactivity and being unable to pull my weight in a team – she would believe I was not malingering. For me there was nothing like jogging in the morning, doing an honest day's work, and at the end of it having some energy left for other things. I loved my life, and just wanted to be healthy enough to live it, but I could barely even crawl through it then.

Although I confided in a few other people over time, even of the ones who understood or at least sympathised, there was nobody with a magic wand, so I was on my own with it. I adjusted my diet and daily routines countless times. I spent all I could on supplements and alternative therapies. No matter what I tried, my strength still came and went like the weather; only some days were far more inclement than ever before. If not for the fortress of my spiritual life, there is no knowing how I would have braved the storms of frustration, confusion and humiliation, day after day.

I had already learned that prayers are best offered without attachment to results, as only God can see the multi-dimensional consequences of our pleas. Still it seemed mine lay like so many scraps of cherry blossom at His Feet. I was left to assume I had something to learn through it all, the same way as I had gained more faith through disaster on previous occasions. I was far more afraid than philosophical at the time though.

When I had at least become well enough to work again, I felt like I was dragging a plough behind me. Evenings and weekends were reserved only for repairing and readying myself for another week. I was beside myself by November, and decided to take a holiday as a complete break, hoping that would heal me. I longed to be with my Guru more than anywhere else – to rest and to soak up the balm of his presence – so I booked another flight to New York.

It was the first time I had gone there without company, and outside the throng of Celebrations. The journey was not so taxing, but in such a fragile state, the arrival itself daunted me. As the clouds dispersed and the grid of the city magnified slowly below, I closed my eyes and offered a silent prayer. I wanted to tell the Master inwardly that I had come to him, although I was sure the news would be of little outer consequence.

Blessings. Though I heard it clearly and immediately in my heart, my mind stamped out the sound with doubt. *Blessings*. It came again twice more and would not be extinguished then.

Since the start of the seventies, Sri Chinmoy had conducted twice-weekly meditations at the United Nations headquarters in New York. Those who had been with him for many years could attend; others could ask for special permission, but I was too new even for that. There was almost no chance I would see him that day before he left for Manhattan. If I went straight to Aspiration-Ground, I might make it in time, but the queues for customs and immigration, and then for a taxi, had seemed absurdly long on my other visits. Overwhelmed by even that much complication, I reached again for the quiet sanctum of my heart. A short passage of golden light seemed to appear inside, and I was sure I heard: *The path is clear*. Indeed there was not even a queue at immigration, and my case rolled onto the carousel just as I walked into baggage claim. Customs was similarly deserted, and a fleet of taxis waited outside without a single customer.

I tiptoed into Aspiration-Ground just as the Master had called for a walking meditation. There I doused my cheeks with happy tears, following the slow curve of thirty or forty disciples as they filed into that sunlit space one by one. My Guru was smiling gently to each in blessing from his gazebo, as if with a grand-father's unconditional pride. In secret silence I clasped the smile to my heart and claimed it as my own.

I slept and rested for my remaining days, sometimes taking short walks in the autumn leaves, or browsing the nearby Divine Enterprises. I ate every day at *Annam Brahma*, the restaurant where Sri Chinmoy sometimes entertained dignitaries. It had been closed for cooking our communal meals during Celebrations, so I had only been in the basement, paring fruit or frying mounds of potatoes. I felt like a dignitary myself just to sit at one of the tables, surrounded by my Guru's paintings and photographs and long cases full of his books, eating from the very kitchens where so many of his own meals were prepared.

I learned the Master would visit an airport on Long Island, where he planned to do some weightlifting. As a decathlete in his youth, he always strove to extend his own previous achievements in various sports: not for competition, but as a spiritual disci-pline. He called it 'self-transcendence'. Although he was unable to run by then, he often lifted heavy weights – sometimes in public – to inspire others to reach similarly beyond their own perceived boundaries. On that occasion, a jet plane complete with passengers would be mounted on specially built calf-raise equipment. I was offered a ride to the airport with one of the locals, so I decided to go. I was sure I could bear that much exertion.

After just the drive I actually felt quite dreadful, but seeing my Guru raise that unimaginable weight was strengthening in itself. He made several lifts and was beaming with joy. Someone had given him a pilot's cap and a shirt with gold striped epaulettes that he wore for the camera. He sat in the cockpit for some time, studying the controls with a child's fascination.

Away from the Master on the drive home I was utterly drained again, and felt only a desperate urge to lay out my length on a bed or a couch. That one ardent desire took up all the space in my mind at first, but was then replaced by another with identical power: a craving for coffee ice cream. I was not one for cravings – certainly none of that force – yet I could practically feel its aching sweetness on my tongue. Having already given up most sugar, dairy and caffeine in an attempt to repair my energy, such ingredients usually did not even enter the orbit of my thoughts.

The two desires still juggled themselves in my mind when I opened the car door at home. I imagined the reality of traipsing around the Jamaica delis with my unseasonal request, and realised then how ridiculous it was. I would go straight to bed and forget about it. As I clambered up the steps, someone passed me to leave: the Master was apparently at Aspiration-Ground and there would be prasad. So then there were three competing desires. I did not stop to listen to them arguing with one another; my legs were already carrying me along Normal Road.

As I reached the gate, Sri Chinmoy had just called for prasad, which on that day was a large dessert, like a coffee flavoured tiramisú. It had frozen half solid from being outdoors, and was full of cream and sugar. I put a spoonful to my mouth, and felt completely well right away, even before I had time to register the flavour. It certainly put paid to my craving too. Perhaps without knowing, rather than coffee ice cream, I had craved my Guru's blessing all along. My strength stayed with me faithfully until the following afternoon.

On my last morning, I heard Sri Chinmoy would be at Aspiration-Ground earlier than usual. Typically I arrived so early that nobody was there, so I perched on a patch of wall in the driveway, reading and reflecting. The local girls from Paree's Group were let in as the Master arrived, but I would have to wait with any others until the gate was propped open. My wall was not so hospitable after an hour, so I crossed the road to the deli for some tea. My coins touched the counter and I felt the keenest urge to run back to Aspiration-Ground, as if I could hear my

Guru's voice calling for me. Most of me thought it was ridiculous – some trick of the ego – but I ran anyway, sliding then to a walk by the gate, which had just been drawn open. About half a dozen singers were at the gazebo, looking behind and beckoning to me. The Master had been teaching new songs to them, and asked suddenly if there were any visitors who would like to sing.

'There's Emily, Guru,' said one of them.

'Where is she from?'

'Bristol.'

'Let her come.'

My warm cup lost its charm entirely; I abandoned it on a ledge and ran to my Guru. The sun anointed everything with pure gold, and the yellow leaves flickered as they loosened and fell. The others all had notebooks where they had jotted down his words as they went along. Some had written numbers above them – a shorthand language of notation – others had drawn curves to indicate the rise and fall of the melodies. As I shared a page with one I knew, joy came, then pride came, then attachment came, and I wished I could stand there singing always. However I sullied those moments with my own desires, I knew they had blessed me forever. Labels I had tied to myself over years, and labels I had let others tie onto me, seemed to fall away like spent leaves. I still did not really know who I was, but standing there I was at least not the shy stranger of my childhood. The world and I found a new understanding that day.

13

Marriage and Mountains

You are your world-loving
Mountain-thoughts.
Therefore, God is going to be
Your lifelong Satisfaction-Partner. [13]
—Sri Chinmoy

My autumn sojourn in New York had helped me rest, and served to stock my inner storehouse for the winter, but by spring I was much worse and could not work at all. Banished from the joys of running or serving, singing and meditation became my quiet bastions of hope. At its worst, my state was a living death: the sum of all my energy no more than the blue bud of a flame almost drowning in its own wax, as though it could be extinguished by so much as a draught.

There had been no choice but to leave *Temple-Song-Hearts*, as travelling to London every week had become unthinkable. I had sold my car soon after, because driving felt dangerous: judging speed and distance was far too complex, sometimes even focusing my eyes on the road was a task in itself. I often could not even read a book – the words would seem to waver and spill, making it impossible to juggle a whole sentence at once. I would sometimes find myself stranded in a room unable to move, too proud or resigned to call for help. The rest of the time, shrinking from the harsh movements of the outside world, and too feeble to carry myself into it, I would let my cupboards run down to only biscuits or plain rice. The café had closed down by that time, but I could not have made it that far anyway without the sort of assistance I was too stubborn to seek. Whenever I collected enough strength to walk to the corner shop for a carton of eggs or a box of cereal, the sun on my skin was new and otherworldly. The colours of leaves in the light, the jostle of people in their everyday lives, mesmerised me and gave a moment's release from the drudgery of illness. Everything was so much more real than it had been in my memories.

There were many who would have cared for me had I let them, but I was too embarrassed to show even those in my own home how I had dwindled. It was the Centre Leader – perhaps the most intuitive – who saw through my guises. She slid notepaper and a pen across my kitchen table and had me write a shopping list. That same table looked like Harvest Festival within hours: a cornucopia of fresh leafy greens, and the sort of hearty roots and grains and pulses that would actually form a proper meal for a change. Sparkles of joy brimmed and spilled from the rims of my eyes. It was as though God Himself had shopped for me. Even the side of a can or a box was sacred to the touch, its contents as precious as prasad. I told her so, and she admitted it felt to her as if she had been shopping for God Himself – the care and honour she took in choosing and carrying it were no less than if she were making Heaven's delivery. Why had I hidden myself in self-sufficiency again? When would I learn that oneness is as much in receiving as in serving?

However I treasured human company and kindness, I still had to live through the daily struggles myself, the same way a marathon runner must take each step himself, no matter who pours him drinks from the verges. As on the metal bridge, I was reminded again that when everything is taken away, something still remains, or rather Someone. At least my independence had shown me for sure I was not conjuring the illness with my mind, as the doctor thought. If I had been shirking, I would have been only too happy to stay idle at home, but in reality inaction was the bleakest torment for me. I had also obviously not invented the ailment for sympathy, as I was too ashamed to take comfort in other people's pity. The outer problem was no different for any of that knowledge, but inwardly it was somehow lighter to carry.

Sri Chinmoy taught by his example the ideal of self-transcendence, but he taught meanwhile to respect the body and not to harm that priceless earthly vehicle. For the Master, self-transcendence might mean lifting airplanes; for others it might mean running a marathon; for me it might mean going to the shops, or remaining cheerful while feeling ghastly. Doing what other people did would be dangerous for me – if I used their maps instead of my own, I would be lost. I thus invested all confidence in my Inner Guide. Still it pinched at me when the routes of others seemed so much smoother and clearer than my own. Although I mustered a brave face, I felt desperately sorry for myself as I watched them putting on their running shoes, or as I waved them off for yet another Joy Day that I would have to forego.

Sri Chinmoy also taught by his example never to give up. As if to appease my mind, I did give the medical profession one last try, and was referred to an immunology specialist. Hope does not blossom willingly in the dingy light and sickly air of a hospital, but all that day I felt cradled by some benevolent force. The specialist took more tests than anyone ever had, and interviewed me for a long time, but still came up with nothing.

'I cannot help you,' he said, as if from a script. 'You are in good health according to Western medicine.'

I thought I had not expected him to help, but the words sounded so final and official, like those of a judge wrongly accusing me of some awful crime. The dam of my will could not hold in that many tears.

'Then. What. Can. I. Do?' I made out in small soggy bleats.

'You must go beyond Western limits and turn to Eastern methods, such as yoga and meditation.'

At first I was affronted by his solution: was I not already

doing just that? It seemed he was not telling me anything new, but I soon realised to have what I knew confirmed by a medical specialist was helpful to my mind if not to my body. It was not so much my own effort that was needed, but more faith in spirituality, and a willing acceptance of God's Grace – if indeed He wanted me to be well. I could not afford to fall apart, and I could no longer witness my life's purpose ebbing away with each new breath. I resumed my hatha yoga practice from my teens, I meditated more sincerely than ever before, I looked up ancient Sanskrit chants for health and practised them daily. I also allowed others to be of service to me, without worrying whether or not they understood me. Of all the medicines, that was the most difficult to take, as it meant swallowing huge dry hunks of pride at the same time.

I was back in the office by summer: a victory I had thought may never come to pass. My colleagues welcomed me as if I had returned from the dead, which did not feel far off the truth. Despite my best efforts, I was simply not as capable as I had been though, and soon realised I was nowhere near competent enough to command my salary: almost twice that which I had started on two years before. Although I had recouped the losses from the fire, I was still swamped in debt. If I could hold down a job properly instead of clinging to some unreachable standard, I would have a chance of paying off the money over time. I decided to move on with honour and dignity, rather than waiting to be asked to leave.

Run and Become was to open a new branch, fifty miles away in Cardiff, and needed sales assistants. It was obvious I no longer had the stamina and swiftness of mind to programme databases and attend executive meetings, but I was sure I could manage to work in a shop, especially in the vibrant and nourishing atmosphere of a Divine Enterprise. Although it was frightening to let go what I saw as a promising career, from the day I decided to make that change, I never looked back. I trained in the London shop over autumn and winter, sharing a room in Pimlico with one of the other assistants, thus walking the same way to work on Victoria Street as I had done so many times as a very different assistant. The route and title were the same, but I could not have been less similar to the girl who first squeezed out of the underground four years earlier.

New Year never seemed significant enough before I started my spiritual journey. The stroke of midnight always augured only disappointment, whichever city I happened to be in. Every year I wondered why I had ended up rolling drunk again, outside under icy rain, in a short skirt and with no coat or hat, milling through crowds of people who were mostly strangers, and who were probably also wondering what they were doing there in the icy rain without a coat. New Year's Day itself was always just another hangover, only longer and more miserable than a normal one.

As a disciple I first started looking forward to each New Year. A few weeks beforehand, Sri Chinmoy would usually give a message – like a prayer for the months ahead – and at the turn of the year itself there would be a special meditation. For those not able to be with him outwardly, there were extra meditations at the Centres around the world. New Year was a chance to refresh one's dedication to spirituality, to forgive and forget one's past mistakes or broken promises, and to start again. The turn of a millennium was infinitely more poignant, and I was only glad to enter it at least with angelic intentions rather than alcoholic ones. Disciples came to London from all over Europe for a huge gala Joy Day. I was in the perfect place for such a signal event, and in much better health to launch into it than I would have been a few months before. I felt my life was beginning again in earnest.

* * *

Run and Become opened in Cardiff at the start of March. Stories of our new shop travelled deeper into the mountains of Wales, and demand for our services blossomed. Not once did I miss my office job; I was spiritually richer in a Divine Enterprise, and even materially I was better off than I had ever been.

I loved it most when the busyness meant the floor could not be seen for customers and their extended family members, assorted shoes and their cardboard boxes, shopping bags, used socks and crouching members of staff. I could only think about giving then, and not about me, so there could be the deepest sense of peace in that chaos. The customers gave me more than they knew: with their enthusiasm, or even just with their presence. Runners are a sunny species. I might say the same things as I had heard leave my mouth twenty times in any week, but to them it was new, relevant, fascinating, exciting even, and thus it was new for me.

At the start of September we would hear a daily chorus from them: the tone dejected from neglect, but still with a Welsh melody. They had come the week before, by bus or car or train, all the way from Pontypridd or Cwmbran, Blaenavon or Abergavenny, and we were closed. Their mother or brother, coach or doctor had told them they must not go anywhere other than Run and Become for a 'tidy pair of daps' – a good pair of running shoes. They would soon realise they were pleased we were back from New York, rather than cross. I had to admit I had missed them too. Their pleading or resolute expressions were always endearing enough to coax me out of the jetlag zone and away from my paper cup of latte. When we told them some of us had run races there, they would be so absorbed by the finishing times, or so fondly immersed in their own race memories, they would soon forget their wasted journeys; they would already be rolling up their suit trousers, pulling up their socks, entrusting their shopping to us, and running up and down the pavement outside to test their daps. The customers may not have known what was different about us, except that we closed for holidays twice a year. Still they seemed to feel something meaningful beneath the frenzy. Outwardly it always felt like a muddle, and especially after being shut for a while.

'Can I have this in a thirteen / in green / when I get paid?'

'Can I leave my bike / pushchair / dog by the door?'

'Do you sell cricket shoes / umbrellas / swimming goggles / rugby tickets / phone cards?"

I did not need to go anywhere to learn; people came in every day to teach me something new, or to hint at things forgotten. Sincerity would come from a screaming toddler beating a fist on the floor. A teenage sprinter would remind me that confidence is a choice. An amputee: courage. A widow: perseverance.

The Shoelace Man visited the shop occasionally too. We did not know his name, or where he came from, or where he went. He did not stay long, and he never deviated from his script. His eyes were most memorable – a rare transparent blue, looking out as if from a dream. A child's smile sat in a bed of deep wrinkles, over a chin that was probably shaven a week before. His clothes neither fit him nor went together, but it seemed that was the last thing he would worry about in his serene abstraction.

'Can you tie my shoelaces, please?' he always asked.

To one meeting him for the first time, the question needed repetition. Once he was understood, there was no further hesitation – his chosen servant bent down on one knee or two, tying one shoelace or both as required. He spoke politely and seemingly without the concern of rejection, as if asking a family member. He smiled constantly, but the laces created a frown on the face of their fastener, as they were quite thin and short.

Then he always said, 'Thank you,' and turned to leave.

Three of us once had a discussion amongst ourselves, having each encountered him individually.

'Have you met the Shoelace Man?'

'Yes! Did you do a double bow?'

'No, I thought he might find it difficult to undo.'

'But it would come undone more quickly by itself.'

'What if he can't undo them himself?'

'He could ask someone.'

'What if there isn't anyone at home when he wants to take off his shoes?'

'Maybe he can untie them, but not tie them.'

'Maybe he can tie them even, but he just likes someone else to do it.'

'Why didn't you ask him what sort of bow he wanted?'

'I didn't think of it at the time.'

'I asked.'

'What did he say? I'll know for next time.'

'Nothing, he just smiled.'

We never knew whether he only came to us. Maybe he went everywhere, or maybe he thought as we sold shoes we would do the finest job of tying his laces. We all peeped out smiling when he arrived, wondering who would be chosen for the task, and watching the sweet exchange.

There is only so much busyness one can take though, however satisfying hard work is. At the end of a day there was nothing better than being around people who knew me back to front and inside out, eating fresh katchuri at an Indian diner, drinking too much chai because it was just too delicious not to, laughing too loud because there was only us around, buying a heavy boxful of too many Indian sweets for Centre night because they were too beautiful to leave behind. Then sitting by myself in my haven home: meditating, singing, and just watching the sky, remembering how I fit into it all, and which aspects of me mattered most.

* * *

After a year, my strength began yielding to the exertion of our flourishing shop, and commuting three hours a day between

England and Wales seemed a waste of my scant supplies. Both my flat mates were looking to move from our Bristol home – one back to Spain, and one nearer her new job – so I set out to look at Welsh property. There were no girls in the Cardiff Centre who needed to share, and I felt rather too delicate to move in with strangers, so I wanted a small place where I could live alone, and where I could put up visiting workers when necessary.

I arranged to have a message given to Sri Chinmoy, letting him know my new ideas. Those outwardly closest to him might seek his advice or blessings on much smaller things than moving to another city, but others like me would usually only tell him of the most significant events and life changes. Sometimes he would respond, and sometimes not. Although I knew my Inner Guide was always with me, there was a tangible comfort in telling the outer one too. I did not want to trouble him with my health problems, but I mentioned them as a context for my move, harbouring a secret hope that he would give me some outer guidance, or at least a hint of how to improve. He sent back a message of blessings for the plans, and surprised me with concern for my finances. Health was not mentioned, so I could only assume all was going according to God's Will in that department, however it went against my own.

Just as before, I only viewed one flat: in Canton, half an hour's walk from the shop. It looked strangely familiar from the photograph, as if I remembered it from the future instead of the past. I was already certain it was right when I stepped into the hallway, but to satisfy my curiosity, and perhaps to convince the agent I was not crazy, I gave the rest of the rooms a perfunctory glance. It was on the ground floor of a two-storey block, small and narrow yet well organised, a little like a moored boat. At the front was the bedroom, with a cupboard under the stairs of the flat above: perfect as a bijou meditation room if I took the door off. A modest living room was at the back, with a galley kitchen at one end, and a back door at the other.

Even though my mind was sure the flat was due to be mine, it was the rotting and peeling back door that conquered my heart. It led into a square yard, fenced on two sides and walled on the others: just a wilderness of grey concrete, with a raised border of mud and some abandoned pots. I knew with a little love it could be magical. The owner was asking fifty-four thousand. All the doors and window frames would need pulling out posthaste and replacing with something less absorbent, so I offered fifty-three. It was accepted by phone before I even set foot back in the road.

I saw several agents in Bristol before choosing one to sell for me. My existing flat had a new coat of white paint, and everything was kept almost surgically clean while people came to value it. I employed an architect to draw up plans for converting the loft, and had a certificate from the council giving permission. The drawings were mounted next to a vase of simple lilies in the hall, in the hope of capturing passing imaginations. As prices had shot up since I bought it, most thought I would get around sixty-five thousand. Although that was a princely increase on the forty I had paid for it, after the legal fees, agency fees, and costs of removal, and with my cut in salary, I would still struggle to get a mortgage on my new Welsh home. Suddenly despondent, I had one more agency to invite: a new company with bright white offices and an unusually cheerful receptionist, who sent a salesman round that day. We both started as I answered the door – he had worked at the same phone company as I had two years before, but we had both obviously reached forks in the roads of our respective careers. Perhaps it was that affinity which made him look with a kinder and more creative eye, or maybe he just had a daredevil streak.

'It's tricky to value; there's nothing else like it. I think you could get ninety-five. We could try it at that for a while and see how it goes?'

We tried it at that. It sold for cash at the asking price within four days. After all the fees, not only did I have enough capital to secure my next mortgage, but I also paid off every last penny of debt from my past. With a fond smile, I remembered my Guru's prior concerns, voiced before I even knew what was ahead of me.

I left my mother and stepfather a set of keys before I moved, as they had offered to make my garden for me. I imagined it would look almost the same at first, as the plants would take time to find their shape, but if God Himself had taken a square of His own Garden and laid it where my grey yard had been, it surely would not have looked any different from the way I found it. The walls and fences were painted golden yellow. A table was set for the birds – in the corner where they would feel safest – and a stone bath for them opposite. Each plant was chosen for its easy care and its happiness in that soil. Clematis, honeysuckle and orange-berried pyracantha already marked out their own territory above camellias with chubby pink buds. Two choisya bushes glowed yellow-green in oases of tiny pebbles. The concrete floor had not been grey at all – scrubbed clear of lichen and the silt of years, it glowed in squares of pale gold, like tropic sand. A bench wide enough for two surveyed it all from the nearest corner. I could do nothing but sit there in the morning sun and behold that piece of magic, alive with love given and received. It was my private paradise, for sharing only with God and the birds. I would equally run to that sanctum in both the hard and the happy times to come.

I was done with whitewash, at least for the time being. Most spiritual aspirants would err on the side of clarity and austerity when styling their abodes, and for a while I wanted that too. Although some may have found my choices indulgent, I knew how colour nourished me, and how crucial beauty was to my inspiration. I was coming alive, like a butterfly hatching. When I had decorated to my heart's content, every colour of the rainbow could be seen from a certain place in the hall. The only white room was my little meditation cave under the stairs. I draped it all in plain muslin, including the space where the door had been, and the slanted ceiling where I pinned fairy lights behind like stars. It was my secret Himalaya.

The pattern of the living room spun out from a huge framed print of Sri Krishna, idling on a gilded scarlet dais with Radha, in sumptuous red and gold embroidered silks. They wore innocent smiles, and their eyes glistened with joy. At their feet, decorated with henna and tiny bells, lay an intricate golden flute amongst lotus blossoms. They sat at the heart of a forest whose perfume almost sprang out from the paper. My walls were the colour of a mango's flesh, and the wood like the skin of a tangerine; the curtains were made of red satin saris woven with yellow; I heaped up tasselled cushions of rosy and sunny taffeta with golden borders. The back door – by then a pair of wide sliding windows – was decked with rich scarlet satin, beaded with coloured glass. Each embellishment had been carefully collected and sewn on by my own hand. The only visible white was in a Transcendental Picture by my desk, and a print of Sri Chinmoy's *Golden Boat* drawing in a huge cerise mount and gilt frame.

'What are you *doing*?' the man delivering the fridge had demanded as I was putting on the second coat of mango.

'It's a *living* room,' I returned, 'it wants to look *alive*.'

I thought it quite courageous of him to question me in my own home, but it seemed he could not help himself. I liked that about the Welsh: they were down to earth, and strangers would often speak their minds like family. I was done with English reticence too, at least for the time being.

The first time I had seen images of Sri Krishna, I had found them arrestingly beautiful and familiar, even on the black and white television in my teens. My interest in him was not purely aesthetic though, however I loved the succulent opulence of the Hindu tradition, the heavenly gods and goddesses, and the heroes from the Mahabharata. As Sri Chinmoy had been raised on Hinduism, and I on atheism, I set about studying Hindu texts to know the deities and characters he sometimes referred to in his songs and stories. It was not necessary, but I wanted to discover his world in more detail. I found myself as though transported to a long forgotten home, as fragrances and colours lifted from the words on the pages. I had entered a magical land where impossibility simply did not exist, where honour and goodness were placed above the premium of life itself, but where intense outer beauty and abundance played their own inseparable roles. In that world, life was very much a play, and the earth its luxuriant theatre.

The more I read of Sri Krishna's story, especially as written by Vanamali in *The Play of God*, the more the ancient values of divine love made sense in my own modern spiritual life. Right from the start of my discipleship I knew a worldly marriage was not for me, and I was at peace by then with being single – in terms of having enough company and being taken care of in the world. Still I had left some part of that understanding on the back burner of my heart. There seemed to me an almost imperceptible difference between being single and being unmarried: one sounded strong, but the other had a drop of sadness in it, at once as small and oceanic as a tear. Taking Sri Krishna's story as a metaphor for life, I could at last think of myself as wedded to God the Supreme: not in any shape or idol or literal sense, only in the formless and nameless. As a husband, only He could be enough for me anyway. I did not tell anybody. Perhaps only I needed to make that inner step, and others have their own ways. It would be another two years before I understood why that distinction was personally so important, but the shift in me was in turn tiny and oceanic. It was a new gauge of my consciousness: at my best, my every day would be as auspicious as a day of marriage to God. As a reminder, I had my grandmother's engagement ring adjusted to fit my fourth finger instead of the third where it had been living until then. There was something even in the diamond itself that fascinated me anew.

When I then came across romance in the world – on billboards and movie trailers, in train stations and cafés – I neither drew to it nor shied from it, but accepted it for what it was to me: a human interpretation of divine union. From then the divine union was the original, and the human only an attempt to imitate that perfect unearthly bond.

* * *

Having completed four years as a disciple, I could apply for a section of Sri Chinmoy's 'Christmas Trip'. Each winter the Master visited several countries, to spend time with smaller groups of disciples than the crowds who flocked to Celebrations, to take a break from the pressures of New York, and also to offer concerts or meet with dignitaries. The atmosphere was thus closer and less formal, the weather generally far more comfortable than the bite of a New York winter, and the four or five star hotels a world away from a shared floor in Queens. It was a special time of joy for everyone. I would spend two weeks with two hundred other disciples on the Hawaiian island of Kaua'i: green mounds and volcanic ridges, like the spines of dragons snoozing and bathing in the Pacific.

Since long striving to accept the outer distance from my Guru, it was a secret delight to hear him passing my door in the hallway en route to his room, or to see him by chance in the hotel gardens. Of course I still could not approach him, but the Outer Guide was so much more real in those environs, and easier to reconcile with his inner equivalent. I walked on the beach in the early dawn, and did not see another living being. It was the only time I had been alone with the ocean, and I half hoped my Guide would appear in one of his guises. It was more than enough just to be in the function room with him and the disciples though: learning the songs or poems that had come into the world that day, watching him draw on blocks of paper and little objects, or just roaming my inner landscapes of silent meditation.

The Master's soulful seriousness alternated with his cute or joking moods. Disciples put on humorous productions of his stories in the evenings, and he would often tell new ones. He sometimes invented mischievous amusements – presumably for our entertainment, and as a means of giving people sweet memories to carry home with them like souvenirs in their pockets. His new game was to take note of the first three disciples he saw each morning: their expressions, what they were doing, what they wore, and whether they noticed him on his way to his morning walk or drive. He would single them out in the functions and maybe tease them fondly, or laud them for something they had done in the past.

Sending an urgent fax early one morning, I stood alone at the front desk as the Master walked out. While I was still half asleep, he was bright as the morning star, his eyes as swift and keen as an archer's. In the function he had to point to me, as he did not know my name, but he described the colours I had been wearing with endearing accuracy, and noted I had offered him a smile. Later I happened to be in the lobby again when he passed by. As I had only seen him do with others, he added a pause to his journey so he could speak to me. It was sometimes his way to ask questions whose answers he already knew, perhaps because the words were less relevant than any inner communication that might go on. Although he only mentioned smilingly again that he had seen me in the morning, asked my name and Centre, and made a fleeting comment about Wales, those moments comprised an entire world in some deeper and more precious universe.

When the Master told stories in functions, I would often struggle to hear or understand. The inner exchange could meanwhile be all encompassing, the threads of the story then melting on the air. Other times I felt he was looking at me and speaking to me inwardly, even when his eyes were closed or his gaze averted, his attention seemingly on other people and myriad other matters. Although ideally I would also comprehend his stories and teachings outwardly in order for my mind to receive that spiritual nourishment, if I focused only on the Guru whom my mind could grasp – my proximity to him, and the level of attention I received from him – the subtle senses of my heart would recede, just as my treasured inner music did.

Although I wanted to be with the Master whenever I could, it was that first Christmas Trip which left me certain I did not need to speak with him outwardly in order to feel his guidance. In some ways the etiquette and other technicalities that necessarily came with his outer presence were a distraction, at least if I let my thoughts get tangled with them. Until I could be more convinced the mind and ego would not usurp the heart's nourishment, I would not wish to be nearer my Guru in the world than I already was. I did not want to lose the sanctity and directness of his company in my heart, as I had felt before I even knew his name.

Back in Wales, my foster home, I determined to retain as much of the trip's sweetness as I could: mostly through meditating and repeating the songs I had learned. Having been paddling in the Pacific only days before, and wandering around in my shirt-sleeves, the British winter seemed so much greyer and less hospitable than usual. In an attempt to bring more playfulness into my work, and also to grow more gratitude for what was, instead of bemoaning what was not, I instigated one of my colleagues to collect auspicious 'signs' with me throughout the day. We would point out to each other anything remotely portentous and exclaim 'It's a *sign*!' or 'It's *auspicious*!' There was never such a thing as a 'bad sign', and 'inauspiciousness' did not exist. It was all done with a generous pinch of salt, but kept us on the lookout for the sort of lesser miracles we might otherwise have missed.

One 'sign' evolved from the ancient superstition that if a black cat crosses one's path from left to right it bodes well, while from right to left means some peril is looming. The latter simply never happened. If a black cat ever stalked past me from right to left, I would find it had one white foot or something else to disqualify it. I was out for a walk once when a very black cat came pelting towards the path ahead from a garden on my right. In a mischievous mood I calculated that even if I sped up to a run, I could not get there in time to intercept it, but I tried. Just as I approached and had accepted defeat, it smacked headfirst into a wire fence lining the garden that apparently neither of us had seen. The cat was only embarrassed rather than hurt. I counted the event as certain 'proof' that inauspiciousness could not exist.

A tradition began that year amongst the girls in Wales, to climb a mountain as the sun rose on New Year's Day. After my six o'clock meditation, I opened the curtains to see what the year looked like, and a black cat was already padding under a street light in front of me, from left to right. Four of us set out for Caerphilly and the forest drive of Cwmcarn. The streets and houses still lay under a black cloak of night that sheltered countless hangovers from the sun's inspection. We left our car alone by a brook at the bottom and shouldered a knapsack for each to take in turn: books of Welsh legends and *Winnie-The-Pooh*, a flask of hot chocolate with full cream milk and extra melted chocolate, a bottle of bubble solution with a round wand in the lid for blowing through, and a torch just in case.

Twmbarlwm is not quite fourteen hundred feet, but woe-betide anyone who calls a Welsh mountain a hill. Legend says there is a real giant buried under it, and treasure to boot, guarded by swarms of underground bees. The walk was all on road really, except for a last patch of clambering. Everything would start in black, then the different greys peeped out and the colours woke up one by one. By the top, the trees were flames of bronze. England lay out raw and blue in the distant south. The sky ripened fast like a ruddy peach, factories and churches shone like little gold trinkets on a charm bracelet. That first light was always drunk in silence. Then we would sing some hearty tune into the listening clouds, see how far the breeze would take our bubbles without breaking them, warm our bellies with chocolate, and read aloud of other adventures that happened before our own.

That New Year there were seven rainbows, one after another. A couple did not stay long, so they were almost missed, but one remained nearly all the way home. Another made a full circle with only a little gap as if it were chasing its tail. Rainbows were our favourite 'signs'. For Sri Chinmoy they symbolised happiness, progress and success. Seven was also one of his favourite numbers, so we could not have designed a more positive auspice for the months ahead if we had tried.

One year a hard frost ornamented everything in crystals. Everything. Even the dirty things like crisp packets left by picnickers, and the fiddly things like blades of grass. We were more hushed that time in reverence. Once there was such a luxuriant fog we could barely see our own feet. We talked more then to know our bearings, and the bubbles did not like it, but we knew the view was there at the top, and we still sang. Nothing much mattered in good company, as happiness usually came along too.

14

Self-Transcendence

Give and give and give!
Soon you will realise
That self-giving is not
A most difficult task. [14]
—Sri Chinmoy

Although the accommodation in New York was always clean and warm, I soon rented a more permanent room. That way I could go when I liked, and have my own wooden cot bed instead of a mat on the floor. There were four spaces available, so I shared with two workmates from Wales and the girl who had sat behind me in the Albert Hall. She worked at Run and Become in London, and sang in *Temple-Song-Hearts*, so I knew her well and always felt drawn to her company. Our two birthdays were a few days apart, and our artist friend had hers in the same week, so the three of us decided to make an extra visit to America that year, between Celebrations.

People often visited the Master for their birthdays. Sri Chinmoy called the birthday the 'Soul's Day' – according to him the soul comes to us that day to remind us of our life's purpose, and of the promise we made in Heaven before being born into the trammels of the earth and the amnesia of human life. It was thus a time for meditation and soulful reflection, as well as festivities twice as sugary and gift-laden as any in my childhood.

There was to be a celebration of Sri Chinmoy's weightlifting achievements, which happened to fall on the evening before my birthday. I had decided to offer watermelon as prasad, and arrived at Aspiration-Ground in time to prepare it, beneath a little awning by the gate. It was the first time I had ever been by myself there; only one or two were setting up inside. I was in my own private world under the honeyed sun of evening, slicing through thick green rind and ripe redness, absorbed by the scent and simple movement. When I already could not have been happier, my Guru arrived early and passed me at my work with a smile.

Just after ten, the function ended, so the Master called for prasad. As the crates were carried out in long procession, he read aloud a list of the items and the names of those who had given them. There were four birthdays altogether, that day and the next. Sometimes he would invite those who had been disciples for at least seven years to come and meditate with him for a few moments on their Soul's Day. I had only been a disciple five years, but the Master called all four of us to stand in a line before him. Although mine was the following day, I was born just after three in the morning, so it was the exact time of my birth in Britain.

'Which one is from Wales?'

My hand crept upwards.

'Oh *that* girl.'

I did not know what to make of his comment, but there was no time to wonder anyway; I was six feet in front of him, trying to summon my best meditation. Half reclining on a soft blue chair with an even softer blue blanket draped over the back, he smiled gently, with his eyes almost completely closed. I wondered how I would know the turn had come for my blessing, but when it did come, I was left in no doubt: it had the force and fullness of an ocean wave. It was all I could do to remain standing.

On the last of our three birthdays, the artist had to leave early, so only two of us remained. We wandered around the Divine Enterprises, buying treats and gifts for each other and for our friends at home, ending up at *Oneness-Fountain-Heart* restaurant for lunch. It was one of those immaculate days, when the sun shines from inside and out: a day when one asks for the dessert menu. As we were doing just that, the phone rang behind the desk. Even ice cream lost its interest when the waiter handed the receiver to my companion. After a moment of silence she covered her mouth, but still made a noise louder than would normally be heard in a restaurant. Although it seemed to be good news, I was not sure until a while after the phone was set back in its cradle. Sri Chinmoy had invited both of us to join Paree's Group.

The Master was offering a concert for disciples the next morning in a garden some drive away; there was to be a race and a picnic afterwards, just like a Joy Day. He arrived in a striking imperial purple dhoti, the like of which I had never seen. I realised then that every colour seemed to suit him perfectly, however soft or bold. We sat on rugs and scarves in the cool grass of early morning, and meditated with him while the sun climbed trees. He played esraj for half an hour; the strings themselves seemed to cry with a mixture of joy and longing. Then Paree's Group sang, nine of us in a line, we two newcomers at either end. By chance that placed me next to my Guru as he rested under a wide umbrella. It was all too real to be a dream, and far sweeter than any dream I could have conceived.

The Master was back in his grandfatherly form for the afternoon. There were stories and games and barbecues and heaped up dishes of things like potato salad or buttery corn-on-the-cob. We stayed until the shadows yawned and stretched. My cheeks were brushed with sunshine and ached from so much smiling.

* * *

Even by August I was still half convinced there had been a mistake: that I would come to sing in the morning and be politely sent back again, back behind the diaphanous screen of etiquette from whence I came. Forty of us followed in one line as Sri

Chinmoy passed beside the open arena of Aspiration-Ground, then around a small stone fountain of lilies, and into a space known as 'the gully'. Gully seemed to me a plain name for a place of such hallowed enchantment: a channel of tall woodland with a red strip of athletic track running at its base. There was a gentle haze, broken by dapples and sparkled shafts of light. Under that secret canopy it seemed even the highest leaves did not turn restless in the breezes, but fell yellow and silent about us like strips torn off the sun, extinguishing their blaze in shadow.

Time itself seemed to renounce its sovereignty. We stood in four lines, offset from one another so each group could choose a different song. The girl at the furthest end would start, and when that song ended, the next would begin a new one straight away, so all the while four remote melodies could be discerned at varying distance. Where he once would have trained for sprinting, the Master took his exercise then at a brisk walk, with stiff and often bandaged knees, his ears only inches from our Godward songs, his eyes almost closed or half open to confer a blessing as he strode by again and again. I strove for an ever new perfection, searching for a word forgotten, reaching my hearing as wide as it would go, honing the level and pitch of my own sound to weave it seamlessly into the whole, emptying my mind of the strange banal thoughts that had somehow followed me into that paradise.

We filed into Aspiration-Ground, where hundreds had taken their seats. A microphone was brought out and Sri Chinmoy asked for each of us to come forward and start a song; others would join in after the first line. Singing solo was still probably my worst fear of all – especially into a microphone – but my Guru was before me, radiant with strength and poise, so I almost dared not bring such a base impulse as insecurity with me. When my turn came, I felt only the oneness of the girls around me, like a safety net or a comfort blanket. These were the ones I had looked up to for years, yet I felt not an ounce of competition or haughtiness from them: such feelings had only grown roots in the mud of my own jealous mind. In reality there was only sweetness, humility and love. There was only one team, and all of us were in it; anyone's strength or victory belonged to all.

An area was unofficially reserved for us at the front of the bleachers, so we could respond as one if the Master called us. He would often start the evenings by walking or cycling around the dusted floor of Aspiration-Ground in deep meditation, and sometimes we would be invited to sing at the edges in two or more groups. There were many opportunities to puff myself with pride, and convince myself I was better than others, because of the attention and privileges I was enjoying. Naturally such thoughts sometimes wormed into me when I was tired or otherwise not at my best. Usually there was no space in my thoughts to wonder what other people were doing or thinking though; not even to note that the sun was especially hot, or the rain especially wet. Focussing on my Guru's activities and meditations, on my kinship with the other girls in the group, and on stretching my own spiritual standards, comprised more than enough occupation. There were simply two levels of kinship – a wider one and a closer one – the way one can live in a city and a country at the same time. I knew from years on the outskirts of that city that I was not inside it because I deserved it, but because it provided the conditions in which I could blossom fastest.

* * *

Although I could work and do everyday things at that time, my only exercise was walking, usually as a commute to the shop. While I was glad for even that much fitness, I still felt pangs of longing when I saw anyone running: the rowing team at sprint intervals between the speed bumps on the road, the self-conscious teenager jogging stiffly on the grass, the portly businessman labouring with slow determination. Working in a running shop left no room to escape the reminders of its joys and benefits. The healthy glows and smiles of the customers were enough to show me what I was missing, even if they did not mention it. Remembering my state of living death three years previously was enough to renew my gratefulness though, and enough to move any sadness to a back corner of my mind.

Sri Chinmoy initiated the *Self-Transcendence Marathon* that August, for seven hundred people. It would be several loops around Rockland Lake, an hour's drive away. Many of the entrants were much older than me, or battled with a variety of impairments, but still made the finish line. The air was full of joyous victory at Aspiration-Ground that evening after the race. Mostly I was happy for those who finished, but part of me sulked that I had never completed such a distance, and possibly never would.

The runners came in turn to a microphone at the function to announce their finishing times, so we could applaud them: over two hours, over three hours, four hours, five hours, six and beyond. Meanwhile, my oneness still alternated with sulking. Sri Chinmoy then said if there was anyone present who did not run that year for whatever reason, but who would like to run next year, they could pass by him for a blessing. Although I had not run a mile all year, and could not even imagine doing so, I certainly wanted to run a marathon, so I was one of the first to go. He meditated keenly on each one of us as we passed, and I felt an untapped strength blooming inside me.

From his own hard-earned experience of twenty-two marathons, the Master offered us encouragement and training tips over the microphone as we took prasad, urging us as always not to harm or endanger ourselves, only to stretch a little further every day beyond any limitations that were merely self-imposed. For me most of his words were only pipe dreams, but as I touched my fingers to the prasad I heard, 'Start tomorrow, run two miles.'

It was not directed at me, but to everyone. It was not an instruction even, but a suggestion for those daunted by the ultimate goal. I pinned only that sentence to the corkboard of my mind, and kept the rest in a little pocket somewhere. I would try it, just that once. If I felt worse after one minute or one mile, I would stop immediately and know it was not for me. If by some miracle, conferred by my Guru's blessing, I could complete two miles at any pace, perhaps I could also continue beyond that distance.

I had not brought running shoes or clothes with me from home, so straight after dawn the next morning when nobody would see, I took out a t-shirt, the trail boots I had worn on the plane, and some checked shorts that were actually pyjamas, then jogged very slowly to the end of the road. Apart from feeling self-conscious, even though nobody was looking, I was fine. I lumbered over another two blocks, and turned around, not wanting to stray too far from home just in case. I was fine. I had no idea how many times I would need to repeat that distance to cover two miles – at my doddering pace, I guessed twenty-five minutes would do, so I called it twenty-seven to be certain. I was somewhat short of breath, but I was fine. I realised only then how strange it was to be fine. I never usually felt fine even when sitting in a chair; tolerably well had become the norm. The remnants of my ailments had vanished.

From that day until the marathon the following year I retained my long-lost health. Ensuring I ate well and took enough rest, I gradually added steps to my weekly journey, and an image of the finish line grew in clarity. It was as if my Guru jogged beside me in all my marathon training-runs, like a silent coach. I felt the joy and freedom of running itself and also the miracle that every step symbolised: through his blessing, God's Grace seemed to have cured me of a stubborn and mysterious illness.

At the start of the marathon voyage itself, Sri Chinmoy

meditated with the mass of entrants from a little platform, and offered a message of encouragement. He beamed and clapped for everyone then, but I imagined it was all for me: for having the faith and courage to start something that had seemed impossible only a year before. I saw the Master sitting at the finish line while I turned my nine loops of the lake. He called some people to congratulate them as they completed the distance, and to have a picture taken with him. If ever I caught him glancing towards me, he looked away immediately. As I grew more tired, I became increasingly fractious and focussed only on the outer circumstances: on my physical discomfort and the fact that my running coach had chosen to ignore me. I was apparently alone with the challenge. I finished just after five and half hours, but I felt nothing, not even relief. Far from calling me over for a photograph, my Guru was on the phone as I passed him for the last time, frowning and looking the other way. Finishing was a pale triumph after the treasured elations of training. It was a miracle, but even a miracle did not feel like enough.

Inwardly it did not take me long to dust myself off after that first marathon, and to see my mistakes. Although it took some time longer to recover physically, God's Grace still seemed to be shining, and I began to imagine entering the same one a year later. I was still cautious of exertion, and my initial zeal was somewhat tarnished, but as the saying goes amongst runners: life is as good as your last run. I knew in a running sense I could not let my first marathon memory also be my last, and the only way to delete it would be to replace it with a better one. Running seemed tied with parallel threads to the rest of living. To leave that matter unresolved would be to give up: literally and symbolically.

By the following August I was at least fit enough to try the race again. I aimed just to turn up and do my best, but even turning up was not as simple as I had hoped. Our driver got lost, affording us an extra hour to enjoy the scenery, but winding through country roads at the back of a bus was not my idea of a jaunt, especially not at five in the morning. Bulging with travel sickness, I was only interested in running as far as the nearest bathroom when we eventually arrived. My hair had been tied when I left home, but it decided to loosen itself and get in the way at just the wrong moment. So I then had the task of washing a sticky mess out of it, by only the cold trickle of a hand basin.

A passing megaphone heralded 'Fifteen minutes to the start!' and I decided to laugh, especially knowing I was still at least five minutes from the starting line. Forget warming up, forget stretching, sun block, insect repellent, *Vaseline*, carefully stashing my energy gels, or even tying my laces properly: I just grabbed my personal stereo from the front pocket of my bag as I launched it towards a tree. All attention on the state of my stomach, I was then jogging towards Sri Chinmoy's opening meditation.

'At least I'm here on time,' I thought. 'At least I have my music too.'

'Low Battery,' the music player replied, and closed its eyes.

Other than giving up before I began, my only choice was to get on with it. Eventually I was glad of that start, as it freed me from all expectation. Joy began with me, and it continued to find me from every source: a new battery for my stereo, a cup passed, a smile, a wave, a drummer, a singer, my name called aloud with enthusiasm, an upturned thumb from a faster friend as she passed. I was not alone, but a cell in one thriving organism, spiralling clockwise around the lake.

The energy of the first few laps gave way to tangible peace as the last of us jogged on through the trees. Even in the thickening heat of midday, my happiness seemed separate from my leaden limbs – somewhere in me it could thrive undisturbed. Instead of lapsing to a frown of doggedness, my smile only broadened as the miles passed. I watched the leaves fall in a chorus of beauty, as if describing Sri Chinmoy's piano music on my headphones. Nobody was even in sight then save a twitching squirrel or sailing swan. In the distance, the speckled mass of finishers gradually appeared from a haze beneath the trees, and I cried with the beauty of it.

That night I was one of the last to approach the microphone and announce my time. Still the smile clung to me.

'Six fifty-three.'

'Good, good, *very* good!' exclaimed the Master, with a smile to match my own, nearly bubbling into a chuckle.

The race had taken me almost an hour and a half longer than it had a year before, but the time was immaterial by then. As with singing and as with everything, I was reminded that although perfection is good, purchased at the expense of soulfulness it is almost worthless to me. My second marathon was by far the greater victory: to me, and evidently to my Guru. From then I considered self-transcendence not so much an achievement as a state of being, applicable to any form of effort. Offering the self fully to a task and wanting for nothing in return bore the sweetest rewards in the end.

* * *

Sri Chinmoy came to Britain twice that year, and his visit to Edinburgh fortunately fell on my birthday. After a special function where he met and honoured dignitaries, there was to be a private function for disciples. I spent the whole afternoon dragging a friend around all the florists in the city centre to find what I considered to be the right vase of flowers to give to my Guru on my soul's special day. When our feet were throbbing from the hike, at last I found a plump handful of lilies, freesias and gerberas – my favourites at the time. They were all different shades of pink to match the sari I would wear, arranged in a simple bulb vase. Nobody else might have thought them exceptional, but to me they were potentially perfect. In the hotel lobby, I proceeded to take the imperfect and overly fussy stems away, to leave a rather sparse clutch of sprigs. I trimmed them further and moved them about for another half hour, defying anyone who came within six feet of my craft, and bearing the brunt of more than a little friendly teasing. It was not so much the result I sought, but more the route: the intensity of a working meditation, the striving for Heavenly perfection through an earthly medium. I went to the hall early, and was allowed to place them on a table in the Master's private room, along with a little card.

The table, complete with flowers, was brought into the main room for the second function. Prasad was carried in at the end as usual, with the names of four people who had offered items for their birthdays. The Master called one girl and meditated with her, and then said 'Family, come.' I thought he had said, 'Emily, come,' and although astonished, I stood to go. The friend next to me saved me any further embarrassment by gently pulling me down again. While smiling photographs were taken of the family with their Guru, I just wished I could hide in a hole somewhere. How could I have been so presumptuous? Even as the family returned to their seats, I was still silently chiding myself.

'Emily,' came Sri Chinmoy's voice quite clearly, but I did not trust my ears, 'how many years?'

At last with confirmation from my neighbour, and a few other pairs of eyes on me, I was standing.

'Six, Guru.'

'Only six? Come.'

I came and stood in front of the stage where the family had been, looking up toward the Master's chair, but he said, 'No, come here,' pointing to the table next him. Presumably as I was only one person instead of a group, that was the most practical place for him to confer a blessing. If only I could have flown to a simple happiness on the wings of my heart; instead my mind seemed to present a catalogue of complications. I did not want to be taller than him, but there was no way of lowering myself without blocking my view – the table was covered in drinks and other paraphernalia, and his jacket was folded on a footstool next to that – so my only option was to stand. It was an honour I would only have dared imagine in my dreams, but in reality I just felt the hot self-consciousness of standing on stage before hundreds of people.

The Master had pulled out a gerbera from my minimal arrangement, and his hand rested on the side of the chair with it. We were already meditating. Again the force and fullness of an ocean wave washed into me and around me, so I steeled myself just to stay on my feet. His eyes were the wheeling galaxies I had first seen so many years before. Time and thought dissolved in his smile. He reached the flower up to me, keeping the stem a moment longer so we both were holding it. Then he let go, and bowed his head with folded hands to the Supreme in me, as I had only seen him do with others.

'Usually this is for over seven years,' he said into the microphone. 'This is a special case.'

A special case? Me? On some level I still felt like the strange skinny child who did not fit in the world, someone to bully and misunderstand. It would have been enough for me to consider myself ordinary, but special was in a different universe to any I had visited inside my own skin. I gripped that dear flower in silence as I walked with my companions back to the hotel, dodging crowds of drunks and partygoers, straining to assimilate or understand what had happened, let alone begin believing it.

Eventually a thought arrived as explanation, the same thought that had helped me countless times before: the Guru gives only what is needed, not what is deserved. To proceed up the mountain, I needed to see the Supreme in myself, the self my Guru bowed to, not just the unreachable God on a cloud with a long white beard, not just the clod of inadequacies and imperfections that I called 'self'. In the same way as the Master gave people spiritual names – names of their soul's qualities, high names of gods and goddesses, names of exquisite divinity – to remind them of the divine in themselves, he was reversing patterns in my own self-perception that I had reinforced and let others reinforce for at least a lifetime.

'What can I do to grow into this truth?' I asked him in my heart that night. 'Since you have gone out of your way to teach me, how can I keep this gift of teaching always, and how can I remain grateful for it?'

'Just give and give and give.' came the answer, clearly and immediately.

I knew it must be true, even if it came only from my mind. I strove always to live by my Guru's example, and giving was all he ever did. Just that one tiny maxim was enough instruction. The people I looked up to most, the people I loved most, were the ones who gave and gave, starting with my mother the day I was born.

15

A Soul in Solo

Walk in confidence-hope.
Look, the promise-land
Is eagerly awaiting
Your auspicious arrival. [15]
—Sri Chinmoy

As always, the Master seemed to be operating in many different realms at once, while tending countless details on earth; his inner agility yet more apparent in the relative intimacy of the Christmas Trip. He encouraged a daily intake of innocent enjoyment and entertainment, but never left us time for idleness, lest we lose our capacities or inspiration. He believed there could be no such thing as staying still in the spiritual life – either we go forward, or we roll back to some previous plateau. There was simply no keeping up with his spry leaps across the inner peaks, but we each had our own pace and activity, as though tailored to our personal ascent. A day with him was a world to me. Others had their own simultaneous worlds where it probably seemed he was for them only. Outside the functions, the halls and corridors echoed with his new songs, as different groups practised to perform them. Even if he was not visible to all, he would surely be creating, composing, exercising, or offering his guidance in words and meditation.

Sri Chinmoy had use of an annex to our function room in Singapore, where he could withdraw alone or speak privately with people. Nine members of Paree's Group were present, and would sometimes be invited there to sing, or to take dictation.

Although it was only a side room in a hotel, perhaps used for cocktail parties or storage the rest of the time, the sacredness of Sri Chinmoy's presence followed there like a fragrance. The disciples kept it fastidiously clean, but it was full of the Master's weights and other fitness equipment, pretty notepads, sumptuous artist's papers and pots of different sorts of pens received as gifts – all surrounded by fresh bouquets and vivid prints of Hindu gods and goddesses. Beyond a set of screens draped in fabric and silk flowers, the Master would usually be sitting or reclining on a couch, while one or two boys massaged the pain from his legs and feet. The first girl would approach and pause a short distance away, waiting for him to compose an aphoristic poem for his *Seventy-Seven Thousand Service-Trees* series. She copied it hastily into her notebook and then returned to the back of the line so the next could step forward. Of course he did not need us for any purpose – he could have used an audio recorder, or he could have called for one of his official stenographers, who would no doubt have been far more efficient. Calling us was a way of including us in his activities, and of keeping us alert. He also gave us credit for inspiring him, even with our struggles and imperfections.

Stepping into Sri Chinmoy's creative world was an honour in itself, but it also yielded direct tuition. All of his poems share their source in his meditation, and many speak of far loftier realms than beginners like myself could even imagine. Like the mountain guide, he would join the climb from the foothills though, rather than just calling down directions from the summit. Many of his poems and aphorisms thus speak of inner blindness he had far transcended, but by noting and identifying with our own limited vision, he sought then to widen and brighten our view. Sometimes before composing a poem he would first glance at a sheet of phrases and ideas, sometimes he would retire into a faraway realm, or sometimes he would meditate on the person in front of him. Often a poem dictated in this last way would thus come from one's own life challenges: both question and reply arriving together in one tiny yet penetrating package. As no spiritual challenge is unique to an individual, in addressing our own myriad inner situations, Sri Chinmoy could speak to countless seekers traversing similar ground.

Those who had been disciples for some time might hope to receive a spiritual name. It would happen when Sri Chinmoy saw that the soul was ready, so the date could not be captured by mental wonderings or calculations. He might give notice that it would be received at a certain future time, or it might come unexpectedly. Names would usually be offered towards the end of Celebrations in New York. During functions the Master would sometimes take out a notepad and a few envelopes that were printed like the sky. A whisper would scatter throughout the crowds, and a hallowed silence followed as he called and meditated with each person in turn before passing an envelope. The recipient would go home to meditate and repeat the new name a hundred times before it would be used or told to others. The name itself would be accompanied by Sri Chinmoy's inter-pretation, specific to that person. In rare cases, two people might be given the same name at separate times, but the meanings could be quite different.

At six years I felt an increasing longing to know my soul's true qualities, to have at last an answer to the question *Who am I?* It was not something I had a right to expect, and I knew very well from past experience that focussing too much on the fruition of my hopes is a sure way to lose track of more important things. Still that wish accompanied me everywhere, like constant music in the far distance of all my days. Though I tried not to let it grow wild like a desire, or allow it to put down its roots in prayer, I often caught myself imagining the day when my turn would come: invariably at Aspiration-Ground, wearing my favourite sari, with the rustle of a cool breeze and my friends nearby. I made a special effort to silence that wish while standing before my Guru, but copying down an aphorism at the front of the line one day, I knew my secret was out:

> 'My soul,
> How long do you want
> To remain undiscovered?
> Do you not think it pains me deeply?' [16]

Sri Chinmoy's tender wording left me close to tears all that day. He spoke not on behalf of my sovereign soul, the spark of the Supreme in me; he spoke instead to that very soul from the rest of me, the limited and struggling self who longed to be acquainted with it. His understanding and his plea for me brought a peaceful comfort, but the poem also seemed to form a license for my longing, and I could not so easily drive it out after that.

I enjoyed far more outer contact with the Master than ever before, but there was still a gulf between the inner Guru and the earthly Guru. For the most part it did not trouble me. In my dreams he was like a grandfather as always, and I a presumptuous child: one he almost could not help but indulge. I saw the worldly etiquette as necessary and I followed it to the letter, knowing that distance was not the sum of my connection to him. My Guru seemed more removed from me than from most of the other girls in Paree's Group, if not all of them. It may well have been a reflection of my spiritual standing, but I preferred to assume my soul simply needed that particular handling. With me his manner comprised disinterest at best and irritation at worst, yet I was sure I almost saw his cover crack into a smirk sometimes. It was as though we both were acting out our given roles with straight faces in the theatre of life, only at either end of the same stage.

The Master would often take pauses in his dictation to talk to one girl or another while the rest of us were still present, or to share an anecdote with us all. If ever he decided to speak to me outwardly, it was always done obliquely: instead of asking me something, he would question the girl next to me, and she would reply on my behalf. It was either amusing or baffling depending on the circumstance, but I did not need to understand. Only if he was any other than that way with me did I begin to wonder if something was wrong. When he seemed distant and somewhat dismissive, I came to assume all was well in the world.

Every day brought new reminders that Sri Chinmoy's outer demeanour could not possibly form a gauge of his interior universe. He may be drawing prolifically, while harbouring a head cold. He may look stern and serious, but then dictate a string of humorous poems or read out jokes from a book in the middle of a function. He may seem cosy and almost vulnerable, with a little fleecy hat on crookedly or a loose shoelace that I would long to tie more neatly for him, but the sudden glory of his words would tremble my bones with awe and remind me he was not all we could see of him.

One day the Master seemed to go out of his way to ignore me, such that I was sure he did not even know I was there. Most of the morning he was lying on a platform doing stomach crunches and other exercises. Paree's Group took it in turns to count his repetitions in sets of ten or twenty, and a boy noted them down in a book. Later that day I felt unwell and went to rest, only to find my earlier assumptions could not have been further from the truth.

'Where has Emily gone?' he asked the other girls with surprise and intense concern.

'She's sick, Guru.'

'Are you sure?'

'Yes.'

'I saw her before.'

Meanwhile I was sleeping, but woke up completely recovered.

Sri Chinmoy almost always noticed when one of us was missing and asked after her welfare, even in New York when we were forty or more.

On Christmas Trips we would usually only have short breaks from the hotel, when the Master was out for a drive. As his legs became increasingly painful, he preferred to stay inside, and so we were more likely to be called for dictation. In the afternoons he would sit in the main function room telling stories, composing songs, or giving us poems. Other disciples could stay or go out then, so the room was only partially full. I did not mind that others had more sightseeing or shopping time than we did. The Master seemed to know when we were tired or wanted a trip outside anyway, and indulged us even that girlish trifle. There was a section of the city famous for its sari shops. Although not one for traipsing around, even I was envious of the opulent bargains I had seen other girls displaying to their friends in the lobby.

'Little India is waiting for you!' Sri Chinmoy issued one morning after only a few poems. We were like school children on a snow day then. I was not abroad as a tourist, and I wanted nothing more than to be in my Guru's presence, but somehow recreation was more precious having been withheld and later granted, than if I had gone for a week of only vacationing.

The longing for my name had reached ungainly proportions, and followed me to Solo, Java, for the next part of the trip. I felt I almost could not take another step without knowing my soul's traits, and I had to invent new tricks to help me carry the increasing weight of that wish. One day as we filed into the Master's annex I imagined leaving the wish outside the door in a sack, like an untamed animal. I promised I would let it out to follow me afterwards if it would just stay quiet while I was with my Guru. The Master seemed in a conversational mood. After giving a poem to the girl next to me, he stopped to talk with her about her name. Then he looked away, but motioned his head backwards in my direction.

'*She* has no name.'

I felt prickly red rising in me, knowing I was the only one in the room still with a Western name, but I noticed the corner of a smile in profile.

'Her name is Emily, like Emily Dickinson. When she can prove that she has the soul of Emily Dickinson, then she will get her name.'

He talked at length about the poet, and about his enjoyment of her 'psychic' poetry – poetry of the heart. He went on to include other American poets in his discourse, and was about to start on British ones, but decided to resume composing his own works instead.

While it seemed my Guru had given me a clue as to when I would get my name, I was more puzzled than ever. I did not presume to take any of his comments literally: a man may be said to have the strength of an ox, but that does not make him an ox; a girl may be said to have her mother's eyes, but that does not leave her mother sightless for want of them. I did not assume Sri Chinmoy was telling me I was literally a reincarnation of a poet. It is human nature to imagine oneself as someone significant in a former life – rather Cleopatra than one of her nameless slaves. In the long journey of the soul, where one progresses towards the divine via countless forms and incarnations, whoever I am in this life would logically be a little closer to the goal than any before, so why would I want to cling to some previous existence? I wanted most to know who I am in *this* life, but I could not discern anything from the Master's hint, if it even was a hint. All that day and all that night I studied his words from every angle, yet still felt none the wiser. Was I to write poetry? Was I to live more from my heart? How could I prove something that I did not under-stand? Eventually by morning I decided that if it was a clue, it was that my new name still waited a long way off, so I had better not waste more time craving it.

Others left the function room for lunch. I stayed brooding in my seat while the Master's food was brought to him. It was then that one of his very close disciples called me to the annex. Sri Chinmoy had apparently dictated my name and its meaning to her by phone the night before. There it was, neatly written in her hand, on the simple transparent jotting paper one might find on a hotel desk. I was sweaty and tired and troubled; I was not wearing a sari at all, much less my favourite one. There was no cool breeze, and my friends were not near me. Nothing was at all like my imaginings, and nothing seemed real either. Instead of floating into some exalted state, I was completely consumed with doubts. How could I know the name was really mine if it did not come directly to me?

The moment I heard the root – *mangal* (auspicious) – I was sure. It beat in my heart like a giant gong that rang through all my inner sky. I smiled as she spoke it, then I grinned, and then covered a laugh as the silent words came to mind: 'It's a *sign!*'

Sumangali

She who brings, from the Supreme, auspicious good fortune to all who are around her. Her service to the Absolute must be unconditional, and from His Grace she will shed divine emanations to all. Divine sweetness and goodness emanate from her soul.

Once again the Master had gone so far out of his way to be indirect that I could only take it as the dearest care. I was certainly not aware of having proven anything at all overnight. His prior words still baffled me, but I preferred them that way: there was sport in them, and mystery. I went to my room, showered and put on my favourite sari, then sat down to meditate. There was my inner Guru – encouraging, fond and light-hearted, like a proud grandfather. On some level the truth registered and I beamed with thanks for it, but it would take some time to settle more fully. When I had chanted the unfamiliar word a hundred times, I went straight to the annex, where the girls had been called for dictation. Although the

Master still retained his stoic guise, my first poem began: 'God has infinite Names'. That was my sole outer acknowledgement from him, and it was more than enough.

All the rest of the day and evening I could not meditate. I still did not consciously recognise anything except the root of my name. Instead of reaching a deeper understanding of it though, I only seemed to manifest the antithesis of my soul's qualities. Rather than bringing good fortune, I accidentally insulted people or gave them wrong information; I spilled things on them and bumped into them. Far from a divine augury, I was a human disaster.

The next day the Master did not feel like writing, only drawing. Although of course we were not needed, he found a way to include us in that creative realm too. He first drew birds on frames of different sizes. One by one each girl would wait for the drawing to appear on the glass, and then take it from his hand to be set on a table. The first frames were quite large, then smaller and smaller ones were used, until they were no more than an inch high. It became more difficult to take those ones without brushing the Master's hallowed fingers with my own by mistake. If ever it happened, I chided myself and felt miserable. When the frames were all gone, he started on large sheets of paper, resting on a board that obscured his face. In that silence and simplicity, my name began to grow in me. Standing only inches from my Guru, but unable to see him, I felt as though a giant jewel of light, like a weightless diamond, was turning in my chest. Rays shone out in golden white from all directions. He seemed to be drawing for a long time as I waited, but just as during my birthday blessings, time paused or became irrelevant, and I was only willing myself to stand upright in that power. Eventually he tilted the board with an archer's precision, enough to reveal a brief and secret smile, only to hide it again behind the page. By the time he handed me the drawing, the smile had disappeared: traceless as a drop in a pool. I treasured the brevity and sweetness of that blessing yet more than the public one I had long thought would come to pass: at Aspiration-Ground, with a cool breeze and my friends near me, a wider audience settling into the waiting hush as I held a sky-patterned envelope.

I had bought my Guru a shirt as a gift, to thank him for my name. Although it was admittedly a beautiful shirt – jade green with fine white batik at the edges – what gift could possibly be enough under the circumstances? I wanted to give it to one of the girls who prepared his meals, so she could put it discreetly by his chair before he arrived, but she would not do it; it was customary that as his spiritual grandchildren, girls from Paree's Group must approach the Master and offer gifts personally. For the first time ever, etiquette placed me closer to him than I even wanted to be. Must I disturb him with my trivial gift? I flushed with nerves, especially as I knew there were few opportunities before I left for home.

The Master had decided to dictate to us from a chair outside the function room that day. Having grown tired of the windowless interior, he wanted to be in sunlight. Rows of disciples gathered, standing or sitting on the floor, watching and listening as we approached him one by one to take poems. After some time, he called for our prasad to be laid on the ground near him. He undoubtedly entered a very high meditation then, but I knew my only chance had come. I offered the package towards him gingerly before taking the little milk drink next to his shoes. His face displayed a gradual return to earthly consciousness, perceptible in stages by the change in his expression. It was as though I had rung the doorbell of a very tall house, causing him to climb down several flights of stairs to answer it. I did not want attention then; I wanted to be invisible and undemanding, but in my granddaughter role, I had to trouble him as I would in my dreams. At last he reached out with a smile and thanked me.

The name seemed to fit more snugly every day on my return home. Not that I could imagine living up to Sri Chinmoy's translation on a daily basis, but glimmers of understanding came from unexpected sources. The word that relieved me most was 'goodness'. It meant I would never need to compare myself to those I considered great. It was their job to be towering and radiant like sunflowers. I could be myself, staying by the ground like a daisy or a primrose, and that would be enough.

I discovered that my name in its literal form – auspicious good fortune – is used in India as a description of a woman who is married, and whose husband is still living. Just that knowledge was a source of comfort to me: it seemed to explain why I had needed to resolve the conundrum of being single versus being unmarried. To remain unmarried was in some way inauspicious, and according to me, inauspiciousness could not exist.

I still did not understand the Master's comment about Emily Dickinson, but studying her poems and biographies suffused my own life with light. Although her physical form was often frail and sickly, it harboured a tempest of intensity and creativity. While she was warm and lively with those very close to her, her heart was as fresh and pliable as a child's, and would have perished in the wider world. Solitude was thus not a choice but a necessity. Even when she had a chance of marriage she did not take it, knowing the thin comforts of companionship would cost her far more treasured and luxuriant things in her own secret world. Contrary to her Puritan upbringing, she first found her God in nature. Rather than acquiring the fears of damnation fed to her from books and schools, she presumed an almost outrageous familiarity with Him, even in His formless and formidable Shapes. Her life was a triumph, despite her struggles with illness and with a world she found unbearably insensitive. Seeing that triumph, I could begin my own life anew – instead of considering my uniqueness a burden, it became a certain boon to me from then. I also acquired an urgent love of expression through written words.

16

Masks and Cameras

In rapture of service-dance,
My boat and I sail.
An ancient cosmic mask
I shall unveil. [17]
—Sri Chinmoy

Ironically, after receiving my name, I lost some of my focus. A spiritual name could not automatically negate the less divine and co-operative parts of myself, but I could not simply unlearn the conscious knowledge of my soul's qualities on the days I felt like being grumpy or otherwise ignorant either, so the bar of my behaviour had been permanently raised. Perhaps complacency crept in when I reached that cherished goal, or maybe for me the longing itself was dearer than the prize.

Increasingly I found myself on the spot and in the limelight: two places I tended to avoid at any cost. According to Sri Chinmoy's teachings and my own experience, I knew that weaknesses could not be conquered in one blow; they spiral back again, with increasingly refined disguises. My age-old friend shyness came back to nettle me on the next Christmas Trip in China, and I railed against it like never before. Although I did not avoid people per se, I avoided speaking out in any circumstance, and worried for the opinions of others. Constantly.

Sri Chinmoy sat in the annex of a hotel ballroom, somewhere in Sanya. His legs had become yet more painful, so he allowed new doctors to treat him, but still his creativity flowed on like a mountain stream from the crystal summits of his meditation.

There was barely any space for us to take dictation, so we entered one by one. The air smelled of menthol and cloves, from some relieving substance. There were open bags and bottles, two disciple boys and two local men crouching or sitting, passing things to one another in a low murmur. I entered at my turn and waited in the only space available. While the Master was in discussion about some technical matter, I thought it best not satisfy my curiosity by watching or listening, so I took the time to pray for new verve and illumination.

'To be a God-lover is much easier than to be a God-server.' [18] He said, slowly and deliberately, as though calling from afar.

As I turned to leave, layered memories opened in my mind like the pages of a book: the sense I had in Edinburgh, to give and give and give; the line in my name's meaning, that my service must be unconditional; the way my satisfaction soared in New York when I tried to serve others rather than counting the things I did not have. To be happy, I knew I had to give to the God in others instead of longing to receive. Sri Chinmoy knew very well what it meant to offer one's life in service. To hear him admit that it may be challenging for a beginner gave me strength enough to at least resume my efforts.

Entering one by one became the norm after that, and more often than not, just the Master sat inside the little room. It was the only time I was ever by myself with him. Often he reclined on a couch, resting his legs; except for his modern clothes it could have been a scene from any age. Although the body was present, the rest of him was gone to some other time or realm. The silence was dense as a forest, so I almost did not dare to tread there, even in my stocking feet. The tiny scratch of my pen seemed clamorous.

Sri Chinmoy loved to take boat rides, so a trip was arranged for all of us before we left the coast. On the lower of three decks was a room with a wide door to the outside, where his chair looked out over the South China Sea. Rows of fishing junks butted against one another at the jetty. Dark flags pointed out above turned wooden railings, perched along blunt formidable bows. Families wearing contented smiles moved slowly and talked loudly from smaller vessels, peering out at us from behind piles of netting. Beyond the port was only a wide misty blue, and the ocean seemed to carry the Master new inspiration like a water-bound feast. He reclined there in the passing breeze, composing lilting songs into a microphone. His voice was only melting tenderness and my heart strained to contain its joy.

Sri Chinmoy took to dictating in the main function room at Xiamen, where we settled next. Sometimes he would obviously be traversing distant inner landscapes while composing, so it may be difficult to hear him, or he might trail off half way through a line and ask to be reminded of how far he had got. If he changed a word later in a poem, it may not be clear whether other words should also reflect that change, or should be left as they were. It was thus sometimes necessary to interject, perhaps reading back part of the poem and asking for confirmation on certain words. I dreaded this happening. I was already terrified of being on the spot, even if the poem was perfectly obvious first time. Often there would be only a short pause between poems, so it was not polite to linger. The Master seemed to journey a long way before he spoke at my turn one day, leaving me unsure of a word. I read back the aphorism as clearly as I could, but apparently I was too quiet, so I called out a second time at quite a volume.

'I cannot hear her,' he said to someone near me, seemingly annoyed. I was stumped; he had no such trouble with others whose voices were so soft that I struggled to pick them up myself.

'There is not a single human being who can escape the world's stark criticism.' [19] I roared for a third time.

'Right.'

I thought at first he simply wanted me to make that affirmation, as it was wholly appropriate for me, but the same thing happened again and again with other poems, day after day, until I raged with frustration. Only in my silent fury did I finally realise it was inner volume he was listening for. While outwardly I was bellowing, inside I was still a mouse, feverishly searching for the first chance of cover. We sat in a semi-circle on that day. There was not quite room for us in one line, so I crept forward beside a plant. If I craned my neck a little at my turn I knew I would be able to see him. As he spoke, he leaned back though, his face disappearing behind a large clock, so I had no choice but to stand. The Master was absolutely in another world. He began, repeated a phrase, changed it, went back into another world, said something I could not make out, repeated it and changed it again, and then asked me to read it back to him. The others looked up at me with sympathy while I did my best, one or two laughing gently at my earnest bewilderment. It went on like that for some time. At last the poem made no sense to me at all, and I looked to my friends for confirmation. Shrugs and shaking heads answered me. I asked the Master if I could check it, wincing as he perceptibly climbed down flights of stairs to answer the call of the earthly doorbell. Instead of bellowing, I read it back with confidence and at a natural volume. He seemed almost disheartened at having to craft his otherworldly wanderings using only the primitive tools of English, but at least I did not seem to be the cause of any irritation, and he gave me then two very clear and compact sentences. My theory had worked, and the game of inner versus outer sound was over.

The Master was requesting more and more plays for amusement in the evening functions. I usually hid whenever the subject came up, leaving directing and even bit-parts of acting to those with more pizzazz, but as always my Guru's aphorisms helped fine-tune my perceptions:

'Do not be jealous of others' talents. Use your own talents. God will be highly pleased with you.' [20] he dictated one morning.

Admittedly I was jealous of those who had the courage to put on plays, because I had not yet addressed that fear in myself. I decided the time had come to face it: by using my own strengths instead of trying to emulate those of others. Near the time of my departure, I found a shop that sold felt pens and card, so I could make paper masks. I wrote a humorous script in rhyming verse from one of Sri Chinmoy's stories – an illustration of divine love, based around Sri Krishna. The parts were to be spoken off-stage for the masked players on their behalf, while they mimed the actions themselves. As a concession to my shyness, everyone was thus effectively hiding for the whole play. The lines could be more elaborate than if they had to be learned by heart, but the oneness between player and speaker still required care and practice.

I was almost certain it would be a disaster, up until the moment it began. A whiteboard was wheeled out to the front of the stage before each function, from which the Master would read out the names of the directors. Although my name was written quite clearly, when he got to it he squinted and frowned and attempted, then finally moved on to the next one. I knew he was playing. It seemed an apt reminder to either speak up, or dissolve once again into the cold obscurity of my own fear. In fact, although so many things could have gone wrong, the night was laden with magic and miracles, such that we almost could not fail.

'Come and pass by,' called the Master at the end, as a way to honour us. 'Stand in front and take off the masks so everyone can see.' He placed the dumbbell he had been using on the ground so as to join the applause. Not only was the play acceptable by general standards, but even those I revered came heaping their praise on us. I filed up to the front for prasad at the end of the evening, not even hoping for my Guru's glance, when a single syllable reached the microphone: 'Ba' meaning 'good'. It was more than enough for me. *If God can make a director of me, even fleetingly,* I thought, *He really can make anything of anybody.*

The next day I felt more alive than ever, having challenged so much terror. My every sense found an exquisite intensity. I went for a walk at dawn, to say goodbye to China. The public park almost reached saturation point by seven in the morning. A dark tangle of bicycles formed a complex unintentional sculpture at the entrance; three long stone hoops created a gateway, each one crested by curled green tiers of roof tiles. As if locked in some darkened oil painting, clusters of Mahjong players converged on stone tables; smoke hung like carded wool between them and the awning of trees above. Some practised Tai Chi alone, and others formed groups. I let myself be mesmerised. While they moved as one body, acutely conscious of one another, their faces betrayed only an inner awareness. Each face was devoid of expression, basking in the serenity of concentration. Tiny children stumped around with overflowing energy as they would anywhere in the world, their fine porcelain faces touched with bloom. Nothing seemed an excuse for inactivity – even the most wizened were out shuffling or stretching with what vigour they had at their disposal. I came across a bamboo thicket, each stem completely covered in graffiti characters, carved into the green skin to reveal yellow. I was glad not to know what it all meant – to see it not as defacement but as ornament.

I continued to the vast and placid scenes of a botanical garden. In the damp breath of morning, huge rounded rocks adorned the edges of a lake. Through mist an ornate summerhouse, open to all sides, jutted out into the depths. All thoughts were suddenly hijacked by its classic splendour. Trees reflected their softened versions in the water; I reflected on a life composed of love and beauty. Within that silence there was space for a fount of gratitude. A steep hill behind invited me to a higher viewpoint. I accepted, and climbed. The town looked toy-like, tall buildings rendered squat. The sun stretched warm hands out to me through a haze broken by branches. There was a tangible stillness beyond the mere lack of movement: a living stillness. I was new again; I knew it then. Letting go the crutches of my daily routines, committing myself to my inner life and my Guru's presence for three weeks, was enough to realign my happiness and inspiration for months and maybe years to come.

* * *

In spring I headed for a significant yet notional point, unmarked by any visible border, where Slovenia joins Austria and Hungary. The forest air smelled of beer and roasting sausages, and through the greenery a cluster of marquees appeared. The sounds of concurrent speeches and performances grew closer. Crowds jostled thickly as I climbed. Some were in national costume; others wore aprons and sold drinks or flags out of crates. My ears still rang from Sri Chinmoy's concert in Lubljana the night before, where I had ended up under a huge speaker, waiting to take the stage: a powerful blessing of music for my heart at least, and a signal honour to sing for the national sporting heroes who had been invited to join the public audience.

An award ceremony called *Lifting Up The World With A Oneness-Heart* was Sri Chinmoy's unique way of celebrating the achievements of others. He would physically lift people above his head as a symbolic act of jubilation – like a sporting cheer in action – and as an extension of his self-transcendence in weightlifting. He lifted thousands of people over the years, of all ages and backgrounds. The equipment thus needed to be sturdy and safe, but transportable to any event. Its ingenious structure was assembled from many metal pieces: custom made by a team of boys in New York, as were many other types of apparatus, built to accommodate the Master's ever-evolving feats of strength.

Ten countries were to join the European Union that day, and Sri Chinmoy had come from New York for the occasion. From all three nations whose borders met at that point, mayors and members of parliament were to be lifted. They took their turn at climbing narrow steps to the platform, individually or in twos and threes. Rising a few inches into the air for a moment by the strength of the Master's arm, some smiled for the cameras, while others appeared inward and reflective. Stepping down again, they took a special medal from Sri Chinmoy one by one.

There was barely any space on the little ledge where the lifting took place; we had to bunch so near as to touch the base of the equipment. In that close-knit throng I thought I caught a glimpse of why the Master had travelled so far to some remote forest track, full of commotion and unfragrant air. That close to him and to other disciples, I felt a tangible oneness unlike any other. It spread as though to the dignitaries and then to the crowds, speeding out to the furthest borders of all three countries and beyond.

Less than an hour before, the Master was inspired to write a song to mark the day. Although we had almost no time to learn it, suddenly we were singing all the seven lines anyway: for the crowds and guests and television cameras. There was nowhere to hide, and no point searching for excuses. If nothing else, some poise and flexibility was forced to the fore in such situations. It was touching to be trusted by my Guru to represent him in public, but it took some nerve to try and keep up with him.

A plaque was unveiled, and the Master gave a presentation in the main marquee, then we all dispersed to find our buses. I was standing by the track, reeling from the power of it all, when Sri Chinmoy was driven slowly down the hill beside me, talking on the phone with the window down. He looked into my eyes for a moment – deliberately, as though telling me something, but I would never find out what it was. He had already embarked on his next activity before I began to absorb the one that had just happened.

* * *

'Your birthday?' Sri Chinmoy asked through the car window outside Aspiration-Ground a few weeks later.

'Yes Guru, tomorrow.'

'Tomorrow,' he said firmly with a nod, and smiled wide. Closing his eyes for a moment in meditation he handed me a large foil-wrapped cookie, and the next girl stepped forward.

I stood at the same place the following day, in a sari that matched my prasad. I had made little paper boxes at home for our group, printed around the edges with decorations and an auspicious aphorism by the Master. They were filled with sweets in lilac wrapping and layers of matching tissue, sealed with a taffeta ribbon.

'Your birthday today?' he asked. The boxes had been passed to him from his driver, and were piled on his lap in a bag.

'Yes, Guru.'

'*Very* good,' he said, with more kindness than I could bear, as though I had done something terribly brave by being born. He held a box for hours before handing it to me, or so it seemed: my heart had stretched into timelessness. His eyes were closed, but in those moments, inches from him, nobody and nothing existed except we two, joined as though by some immortal strength.

Treading the corridors of the United Nations headquarters that afternoon, I felt I was travelling through the arteries of the world. My journey's end was a small theatre where the Master was to conduct his twice-weekly meditation. On stage, a chair waited beside a narrow desk that held only a candle and a flower. Sri Chinmoy entered in a glowing yellow dhoti. He seated himself in a silence that seemed to grow into a long crescendo of peace over fifteen minutes. A small group of disciples came forward to sing, and the Master composed four new poems. As though his inner offering could not have been enough nourishment, he took truffles wrapped in foil one by one from a tray with his neat brown fingers, and dropped them into the hands of each of us as we left.

Three days later, eight of us sang in the gully, and the Master gave us prasad from the car. I beamed with joy and oneness as he offered my English friend a blessing meditation for her birthday, just as I had received. A boy was standing nearby with a camera, so he kindly thought to make a souvenir photograph. The tiniest flicker of envy sped across my mind like the shadow of a bird: there had been no camera for my birthday. I was last in line, so I had ample time to chase out the ridiculous thought before I reached my Guru. As I approached, he turned away to one of the boys. Thinking he had resumed his old sport of ignoring me, I stood back a polite distance to let him speak and perhaps even to give away the prasad I had hoped was mine. Then I realised it was the boy with the camera, and the Master was asking him to take a photograph. A cardboard tube of biscuits came through the window toward me, but his hand kept it fast for a moment as I held the closer side. Whether he remembered there had been no camera for my birthday, or had read my unseemly desire from the back of the line, it was an equally sweet indulgence.

* * *

I was dreading the bus to Buffalo a year later. I had heard we would go overnight on the way there, and back the next night after the concert. Having already spent a night on a bus from Wales to Heathrow, that would make three bus nights in a row. It sounded worse than camping, but it was my birthday, and I was determined it would be a happy one.

We were leaving in the morning after all, and Sri Chinmoy was to make the eight-hour journey with us, so the wretched trek in my mind became an idyllic family outing in reality. The Master composed poems, reading through a microphone behind the driver's seat, and we all repeated them aloud in unison. The freshness of the creations and depth of their meanings, accompanied by the concentration of hearing and correctly repeating the words, was at once clarifying and elevating. He then sang a hundred of his most familiar songs, and we all joined in. There were many stops along the way; at one the Master offered a huge prasad like a meal in itself, meditating at the front of the bus while we filed past outside and picnicked under the trees. Other times, a little bag of sweets or biscuits was placed on the seat opposite him, and we stumbled down the moving bus to take one in turn. The sun blessed us profusely. America shone in all her summer finery and ample beauty. Time ebbed away as it does in good company, and I did not want the drive to end.

Preserved with meticulous care since the nineteen-twenties, the theatre felt like a walk-in family heirloom. From the illuminated list of events above the entrance to the ornate glass and wooden swing doors, it was like stepping into a black-and-white film. Inside, the velvet seats, sweeping balcony, and intricate ceiling embraced a modest stage, watched over by a space age neon-lit chandelier.

Sri Chinmoy gave sweet and haunting performances on many instruments, but throughout I could not contain my anticipation for the finale. Nestled in the orchestra pit was a *Mighty Wurlitzer* organ, used for music and sound effects in the days of silent movies. The controlling organ itself was tiny, but by means of keyboards and pedals it commanded a fleet of instruments spanning the whole pit. A piano, a vibraphone, drums and a siren were among the players in the remote-controlled orchestra. They created more than just an experience of sound: little light bulbs the size of golf balls, in all different colours, were attached to almost every component of the instruments. The top row of organ keys produced a flurry of bells and accompanying twinkles of light pulsing along the stage.

It was all as though from another world, like a strange and delightful dream, only stranger and more delightful. I had noted before that the Master seemed to suit every possible colour of clothing. I was reminded that he also seemed able to turn his hand to any instrument: from the power of a grand piano to the frolic of a piccolo. Although that organ was entirely new to him, he seemed to thrill at its childlike charm. The sounds and lights were as flocks of imps or fairies, dancing and playing much too quickly to be seen.

It all went very quiet on the bus as we boarded about midnight. One would expect that everyone, perhaps including Sri Chinmoy, would be tired after such a day. The Master did not take a moment's rest though, even after his extensive performance, but took out a book of funny quotes and started reading them over the microphone, chuckling as he went along. I giggled inside, without the energy by then to manifest it as proper laughter. I think everyone else felt the same, but he was undeterred, eventually asking in a voice full of mischief whether anyone was awake. I laughed out loud at last – fondly, at his inexhaustible energy and joy.

I woke at five, already smiling softly as mist covered the huge verdant scenes sweeping by outside. Wildflowers in great clouds added to the gentleness and perfection. The sun hung bright orange with a red rim, as I had never seen it. Later Sri Chinmoy wrote twenty-seven songs, mostly in Bengali, which we all sang together. After prasad I was sure I could not have been happier, but someone was beckoning me to the front of the bus for my birthday blessing. I jogged forward in surprise. My Guru's hand extended past the side of his blanket, signalling for me to sit across the aisle. I looked up to see a camera pointing towards me, and the Master behind it. There was no time to compose myself before the flash went off. I made to leave then anyway, disappointed with my own lack of poise.

'No, stay there.'

He moved back and seemed to take a long time focussing, but that could have been a charade. I felt the same oceanic power as

I had on other birthdays, and was grateful to be seated for it that time. Although the camera came down after two more flashes, he did not look at me without the lens.

'Very good.'

17

Newer York

If you are brave enough
To sing through darkness,
Then light will sing through you
And for you. [21]
—Sri Chinmoy

By winter I was barely strong enough to make it back to Asia. My health had crumbled again, so I could no longer work, but I was not ready to accept another collapse like before. In addition to my familiar incapacity, I seemed to have developed chronic pain, mostly in my head and shoulders, or sometimes in my whole body – even the tiny muscles of my fingers and toes. In denying my condition, hoping day after day that I would miraculously recover, I probably only drove it deeper. The struggle seemed milder in the tropic charm of Malaysia and in the balm of the Master's presence, but by the time I reached home again, I was limp as a doll. Despite my longing to be of use, I only dragged slower through my days, selfish by default in order to preserve my scant reserves.

Although the lavish care of my family and friends saw me to August, I knew by then I had to face reality: I must exercise my oneness by receiving, as there was simply nothing left to give. Swallowing a dry morsel of pride, I asked my mother if I could come back to her. She sounded only relieved that I had accepted the illness, and could thus perhaps begin to heal. For the first time ever, I realised how I missed my beloved England, instead of trying to escape it as I had done since before I could remember.

There was a small Sri Chinmoy Centre in York where I could attend meditations twice a week. Once again I sought my Guru's blessings for the move, and prepared for a new life.

In previous months, when I had still been able to work, but could not do many of the other things I loved – like running, or singing for the public – I had filled the gap by learning how to build and look after websites. It was a pastime and a means of additional service then, but by the time I went back to York, it was the only occupation I could manage at all, and still only for brief stretches. Although the channel of my usefulness had narrowed, at least it had not sealed up altogether, so I was all the more glad of that technical and artistic outlet. It was the best hope of supporting myself over time, and it also seemed to match my soul's purpose of giving to all those around me: potentially to the wide world.

Sri Chinmoy's maxim 'Never give up!' turned in my mind and heart like a mantra as I packed away my things, leaving Wales for a new scene in the play of life whose script I had yet to see and learn. Whatever I endured, I remembered what unknowable pain and incapacity I had escaped one August day on the westbound M5. It was ten years since I had returned from Thailand and first struggled through a bout of some peculiar illness, thinking I would bounce back in time, but a decade on I was no nearer understanding it. I could prod at reasons for the ebb and swell of my strength, but every theory of mine or anyone else's was soon proven wrong. If there was either cause or pattern, it was apparently beyond any human power to expose it. My health was entirely in God's Hands, as changeable and ungovernable as the weather. As the saying goes amongst runners: there is no such thing as bad weather, only inappropriate clothing. In the same way, I was determined not to use the inclemency of my health as an excuse for complete inaction, or a cause for complaint. I would simply fit my life as best I could to the inconstancy, weatherproof my days with meditation, and endeavour to retain my smile.

* * *

I had improved somewhat by the next Christmas Trip, which was to begin a manageable flight away in Turkey, then on to Bulgaria. The whole adventure sparkled with new joy and little miracles.

My first roommate would arrive a few days late, so I stayed by myself for a while. One afternoon, I came in to find a single gerbera in a tiny vase on the desk. It seemed to have been put there very deliberately, with a neat array of foliage behind, but without a card. It was not a special day for me. I wondered if the hotel had put one in each room for hospitality, but I asked a few friends and they had received no such floral gesture. I waited to see if someone had sent it on a whim or in playfulness, knowing it was my favourite, but nobody owned up. Though it was a small thing, often the small things mean the most. As the days unfolded, I realised that whoever had sent it had done so unconditionally. However it came there outwardly, I decided it had come from God, and I treasured it all the more.

Sri Chinmoy loved circuses. There happened to be a Mongolian troupe in a tent along the road from our hotel in Antalya, and the Master decided we would all go along one evening. We took two entire sides of the audience, bundled up against the cold on plastic garden chairs. I arrived a little late, to find there was only one seat left in the area where my singing friends had gathered: behind and to the side of my Guru's place. The ground was only gravel, the primary coloured canvas of the tent was tired and grubby, but the Master's armchair had been brought in and draped with clean white blankets. I could not see him, only the peak of his hat, and beyond his sleeve the fingers of a glove: slightly too long for the neat little fingers they contained. For an hour or more we watched the performers in their sparkles and silks, beaming smiles and ruddy cheeks, jumping and flipping and balancing with athletic ease. To be so near my Guru, to enjoy the same innocent spectacle in the same earthly time, was a waking dream to me.

I had amused myself at home by preparing a rhyming play, that time with proper painted masks and props. I was glad to bring some enjoyment to the players and the audience, even with my sparse energy, so I wrote a second story for fun while I was there, using the same costumes. I slept longer than usual the morning after the second performance, and dreamed of my Guru. He was speaking to me in Bengali, the way an adult would to a tiny child – knowing the meaning could not be grasped, but conveying such joyous affection in his smile and eyes that the words did not seem to matter.

One of Sri Chinmoy's closest disciples approached me later that day in the lobby. She said how much she had enjoyed the play, and that she had brought up the subject with the Master in the morning, as he went for his early drive.

'Guru, isn't she brilliant!' she had said to him.

Imitating his response, she nodded back her head in the same dismissive way as he had done the day before I received my name.

'Tcha!' he had replied. 'They are all *my* stories!'

She pressed him further to praise my interpretations, but he did not yield.

'They are my stories, she is writing from *my* stories,' he volleyed, apparently with mounting irritation, and then changed the subject.

She seemed apologetic, as though her efforts had failed. Little did she know how much sweetness I juiced from those words and descriptions though: far more than if my Guru had conceded to give me credit, or had made an example of me in public. Any outer acknowledgement would have seemed synthetic compared to the fondness I had felt in my dream – a dream that was probably taking place at the same time as the seemingly dismissive outer conversation. To me the whole incident was the dearest proof that my inner connection to him was all that mattered. Far from being disappointed, I only laughed softly and secretly, over and again. It was simply his way with me, and I would not have exchanged it for any other way.

Most days the Master would call Paree's Group in the functions and give us special prasad, as well as the group of boys – similar in number – who attended him at Aspiration-Ground and during trips. He would often throw the items for us each to catch in turn, and seemed to enjoy the sport immensely. While it was a signal honour to receive prasad by hand, the mere thought of it caused my own palms to glisten and my heart to launch into a gallop. I was simply an awful catch. However I prayed and concentrated I would almost always drop the precious offering from my Guru's hand, no matter its shape or the way it was thrown. I was not the only one who missed – some were notorious for dropping, and others would do so occasionally. The Master was still a nimble sportsman even then. Sometimes with a mischievous glint in his eye, he would make a person run or jump for fun by throwing out of bounds. He usually gently teased anyone who missed, but with me he said nothing, presumably because I was already plainly mortified.

One girl in our group had a birthday in Bulgaria, and had brought some chocolates from home as our prasad. They were fine pralines wrapped in pleated foils of all different colours, tied with a co-ordinating ribbon and a dainty silk flower.

'Please, please do not drop these!' implored the Master. 'Very special, very beautiful prasad.'

In line I prayed intensely for the capacity. Just once could I not do such a simple thing? I stepped up and held my breath, pinning my eyes like a kestrel to the tiny parcel as it left my Guru's hand. Not only did I miss, but also in lunging forward to catch it, I kicked it under a display of plants. The only choice was to crouch and grovel for it in front of everyone, while the whole line waited behind me. In the scheme of things it was a small incident, but at the time I made it a symbol of a much wider uselessness. I returned to my seat on the fourth row and hung my head in tears, sulking with God for not hearing my plea, and wishing the ground would embrace me.

'Ten hearts are left. Oho! Who will get them?' The Master's chuckles were enough for me to glance up, before delving again into the swamps of my new misery. There were similar chocolates, heart-shaped and all in red foil, arranged beautifully in a separate box. He called out the names of those along the front row, and threw a pleated heart to each of their seats.

'Two more only,' he said, and called to someone further back. Then there was only one.

Even with my head bent as low as it would go, I noticed the two girls in front of me diving apart to avoid something as it whistled past their ears. I felt a sudden sting on my forearm. The Master had thrown the last heart, shot like an arrow from a bow, without so much as a curve in its trajectory. He had not called my name, but my attention had not been needed anyway, since the effort was all his own. A long pink glow showed where the foil had met my skin. The heart was resting where it landed: in the crook of my right arm. From that day I was able to catch any item from my Guru, even those thrown askew in mischief.

Bulgaria had been cold at first; no amount of clothing would stop my teeth from chattering. All had looked empty and somewhat stark, yet each day became a fuller, friendlier blossom than the last. I searched for the rising sun from breakfast on our last morning, but the trees were hiding it. My shawl was already packed away and I wore only a sheer sari and little sandals. I stepped out, folding my arms tightly, my bare toes cringing instinctively, but the assault never came – the air was bright and mild. I followed an overgrown stairway to the sea, where the sun drizzled light like a spilling bowl of nectar, changing constantly beneath the cloud. The sea waves were only little tremors of joy and anticipation. Outer events in that three-week sojourn melted into one fine stream of thanks. The weather's transformation seemed a perfect echo of my own inner renovation in the daily presence of my Guru. It was a year newer than any other I had known, and I felt I was running to greet it like a child.

* * *

Back in my childhood home, I peep into the sunroom and look on the napping faces of those who call me daughter. Tears come from nowhere. There sits sacrifice in two human forms, in two adjacent armchairs. One bore me, one claimed me; both gave so much of their combined lives for the enrichment of mine.

I work in the tiny room that was my brother's – it would not offer him enough space even for visiting, now that he has a family of his own. I will be an aunt again soon, for the second time. I laugh out loud at the adult roles we play, when I still think of us as children. Laughter was never in short supply, even when there was really nothing to laugh about, and still we always seem to find it. We giggled breathlessly over old photographs the last time he came Up North: the hairstyles, outfits and expressions. Silence came suddenly when we reached one of me holding his hand, watching a deer – he knock-kneed in little shorts and a head of curls, I much taller in a yellow pinafore. It struck me anew that families are not born randomly, that maybe they have a depth of significance only the heart can understand.

Is this even the same life? Am I the same girl who moved Up North a quarter century before? These city walls stood for a millennium, but in the wink of time since my teens are they so changed? Through my open window, breezes bring the bells of the Minster, surging like a tide. Strangers smile at me in the road, one, two, three before I realise I was already smiling, and they perhaps politely returning. Was that old cherry tree there in those days too, hurling confetti into a brilliant sky like the mother of some cherished bride? Is that the river inn where once I turned sixteen in a frenzy of loud friends and a cheap euphoria of cider, my feet lolling in the watery green? There are other loud frenzies now, and some look my current age. Is their joy as hollow as my own once was, as fickle as a draught? Are they still wondering: *Is this all? Is this it?* It was not this place that was dull then, it was these eyes that saw it so, and these same eyes that see it perfect now. I am home, and in a city I once thought could never fit me.

There is a building by the railway in town, made into eight little abodes. I saw it in the autumn newspapers, and thought I recognised it as I had done with my Welsh flat. It disappeared again through winter. Now it is back, I show it to my mother, even though we both know I am not earning enough for it yet.

'Come on then, let's go and have a look.'

'But what if I fall in love with it?'

'Just from the outside?'

House prices have further skyrocketed. My home in Cardiff – by now with a plush square of honeysuckle and other greenery at the back – sold for nearly twice what it cost me, but I would only get a one-room studio for the same price in York. Most of the ones in agency photographs look more like hutches or cells than homes, or they are far enough out of town to be called somewhere else. This one is almost sitting on the rail tracks, but it lies only just beyond the city walls. It looks like an old stable, or something transplanted from a farmyard, and aside from the trains it has an almost bucolic air of peace about it.

'Oh dear, it's perfect isn't it?'

'Yes.'

Inside – where we had sworn not to go – is wall-to-wall squalor, but we both already know it is too late to unlove it again. The bathroom suite is so old it must have been put in second hand; a hole in the tub is patched with glue and tape, and there was never a shower at all. Linoleum is stuck down to soggy chipboard that squeaks and bounces. The walls are creamy and shiny, like the skin that forms on hot milk. Up a ladder in the eaves is a square shelf where a bed would fit. Its window cannot remember the last time it was opened; black canvas like a giant pirate's patch is tacked over it with pins. Dark mould crawls up the glass underneath and between its twin panes. Apart from the floorboards, walls and window frames, everything will have to go.

Our matronly financial advisor finds me a back door into some seemingly impossible plan. Providence seems to have everything in hand: I am already signing sheaves of paper covered in numbers and foreign phrases like 'self-certification' and 'stamp duty'. Luckily I have always been surrounded by engineers, who have miraculous ideas in the middle of the night – for storage or drainage or light fittings – so all I have to think of is colours. Six men come at once with six sets of tools. The floor is covered in dust and cables. The walls are covered in wet plaster and new holes – some in the wrong places – and we all wonder what we have started. We clean and sand, clean and sand and paint. I leave my brother to lay the floor, and my parents to fit an entire kitchen, while I go to celebrate my Guru's birthday in America.

Before I know it, my new home is full of the morning sun, even under the white blinds that veil its skylights like Japanese paper screens. Everything is white in different textures, save the glossy golden floor of shaved bamboo, textiles in leafy yellow greens, and kitchen walls the colour of a Granny Smith apple. I have brought home new work and my strength is doubled, despite the strains of renovation. Everything is quiet unless a train rumbles by, or the bell ringers practise at the Minster, or the children play outside the nearest school. Everything is clean and new; even inside me there is a twinkling clarity like the sort that comes after a heavy rain. Where did such perfection come from? Is it here to stay?

* * *

'Our Guru is gone to the other world,' comes a voice through the receiver.

It feels like learning to swim; like plunging alone into cold deep water. How am I to bear myself forward? All my strength seems absorbed in merely staying afloat; my struggles have no purchase, but dissolve instead, lost entirely in loose ripples. There is nothing to hold and not enough gravity, yet the sucking weight of my own self forces the breath out of me.

Suddenly I am making the familiar flight to America, but in uncharted circumstances. Muffling sobs that spring up unbidden, I walk down the covered gangway, past the rows of newspapers and clusters of airport workers in fluorescent bibs. The inescapable smell of the airplane interior seeps out of the door, mixed with a blast of jet fuel, and I realise I did not say goodbye. Through all the years I have been to see my Guru, I have said my farewells to him in my heart before departing again, thinking it could be the last time I rest my eyes on him, for any number of reasons. I always took an inner snapshot as he made his way slowly to the side entrance of Aspiration-Ground, tottering like a little child in the latter times and holding on to the gate's frame to steady himself before disappearing into a car. I cannot remember the last bittersweet moment, some time in August Celebrations. Like inauspiciousness, perhaps I simply could not countenance my earthly parting from him. People are piling their coats in the overhead lockers. I buckle the cold metal around my middle and lose myself in memories.

The evening was diamond clear; a white moon reclined behind skeletal trees. One trunk held out many pristine arms and hands of long-petalled blossom in a shower of purity; a canopy of white paper banners reflecting their softness, glimpsed over stone walls. In the still air we waited, each holding a single rose. I caught the scent and felt the cold stem in my hands as my eyes absorbed its colour. All was simple in my mind and sight. I only waited with a band of friends, just a bloom for my senses, preparing to offer my heart in sound. One followed another into the sanctity of Aspiration-Ground. Gravel grinding under foot gave way to the softer powdered floor. Between two stone lions, along a bank of carefully tended spring flowers, the warm scent of hyacinths leapt out from the crisp night. I had felt hints of it in other places dedicated to prayer and meditation, or in simple places of natural beauty – that living stillness, abundant silence, gentle clarity – but those places were homes to other people. I was in my dearest home, my own favourite place in the world, basking in something far beyond the world's mesh and material. There was nowhere else I would be than in that outdoor room, in the vibrant open air, singing with devotion to God, before my Guru who had given my life the wings of its inspiration. That moment was the prize of many hours spent alone in concentration on the songs, many more in company learning the subtleties of the music to sing as if with one voice: beyond individuality, merging sound with sound, breath with breath, far from thought, and into the heart of music itself.

The last thing I remember clearly was the Master receiving treatment from doctors in the early evenings at *Annam Brahma*. Paree's Group was allowed to sit on the floor behind a screen, each taking turns to start a song. It was hot and the restaurant girls made us juices, passing them from hand to hand along the makeshift rows. Sometimes Sri Chinmoy would join in with our singing, or hum along; sometimes he would call out requests. After the session, the screen was folded away and he perched on the edge of the couch with a plastic sack of potato chips, throwing the little packets to each of us as we filed out the door.

I remember the end of one function – possibly my last. It was a typical heavy August night, silent but for the choir of cicadas. The Master was sitting on the longest side of Aspiration-Ground as the tables were brought for prasad. I waited until the crowds had thinned, and went down with the last trickles of girls. Once my arms and hands were laden, I looked up to find my Guru in a serious attitude with eyes wide open, but seeing my smile his own face spread into a particular warm grin, as I had only seen him give to others. I wondered then how strange it was for him to make a special smile for me – that was not usually our way – but he neither checked himself nor broke eye contact until I had moved out of sight. I realise only now that smile was to last me a lifetime: it was not necessarily deserved, but it would need to sustain me until Heaven.

I remember there were gold lockets for sale once in the daytime that August. They contained Transcendental Pictures, and the Master was to bless them. I thought there would be other chances, but I happened to have the exact money in my pocket, given me by a client just moments before. I placed the little pendant on its red velvet pouch and held it up on the flat of my palm for my Guru's blessing. Outwardly a blessing usually comprised a brief gesture of the hand, symbolic of a far deeper inner benediction. The hand that I had always tried so carefully to avoid touching by mistake came straight down on mine though, so I had to rivet my back foot into the ground to stay balanced. It was as though he was reaching through my skin and bone to my very heart, in a final signal of oneness. I already treasured the pendant then; little did I know how precious and singular it would become.

Years ago I remember watching Sri Chinmoy walk down the drive one day and I saw in his face only a living breathing Transcendental Picture. One is a photograph of the other, but I still had not reconciled those seemingly disparate Gurus. Although I never saw it so clearly again, my meditations at home and at the Centre acquired more depth and meaning after that. The difference between knowing logically and feeling from my own experience was at once tiny and immense. From then I was certain that although he would depart the earth one day, my

Guru would not leave me. The Guru and his picture were synonymous; the inner life could not end with the outer form.

Until I had been to New York, I had thought weather – bucketing rain or beating sun or biting cold – had the power to hamper happiness. In time I found that as long as one has a sunhat, or a raincoat, or a pair of good mittens, or sometimes all three in a day, the only resistance is in the killjoy mind. I remember one April morning waiting on the bleachers at Aspiration-Ground for the Master to arrive. It was snowing a little at first, but I had wrapped up cosily and had plenty of songs to learn. Occasionally I trudged across the road to buy hot chocolate. Other than that, I stayed for six hours until I heard for certain that he would not be coming out. By then only a few people remained, and the snow was falling in feathery clumps, yet there in the pure silent softness, my Inner Guru felt so near, and I did not want to leave. That I could meditate so easily without his presence was instruction in itself: instruction that I treasure all the more now, knowing however long I wait on the bleachers, he will not come out again.

Now I stand on the side of Aspiration-Ground where once a fairground carousel turned with stately grace, its passengers perched on exquisite painted animal seats surrounded by all the associated braid and bunting: tiger, deer, buffalo, bull, lion, elephant. Each rider seemed ageless, wearing the smile of a mesmerised child in the glow of shaded sunlight. Dream-like organ music filled the air. Sri Chinmoy reclined, powering the entire apparatus with his feet on two simple pedals.

The night is full of stars and candles, and silence is the only music now. I realise in how many ways he has taught me to rebuild my own innocence. I once thought I had been indelibly defiled by my worldly life and my own mistakes, but instead I am newer by the day. I join the line of white-clad figures, come from around the world to pay their respects to the Master's physical form. There seems yet more love between us all than ever there was before. I take a little flame in a jar and place it by the open casket, but in those silent moments that are only my own, I do not find my Guru lying prone in a satin dhoti. He is gone from that earthly habitat. The tautness of suspense that always hovered around his activities, and around the meteoric flow of his creations, has vanished and can never be recovered. Nothing is gone from Aspiration-Ground though; nothing is gone from the Transcendental Picture; nothing is gone from my heart. Everything is different now, and everything is still the same. He was never to be found or lost like other people anyway. It is as though he always was, and thus ever will be. With that immortal strength beside me and within, I traverse eternity.

* * *

Sweet frankincense –
a clarion scent
a heralding of saints or kings?

Squirrel sprints in gathering
but sun leaps out of clime
breaking its faith with autumn time
One tardy bee labours long
humming low a working song
treading cheery and meticulous

Vines thread red necklaces
Jars of flame glitter fast amongst petals
Alive! Alive! A peace of ages settles
deep inside this verdant plush
Some rearrange in gentle rush
all in white with ardent care
Others sing into the empty air

Hush! Hush! go the footfalls soft on gravel
In me memories unravel –
long tapes of smiling scenes
from in this leafy room

Tap Tap
Tap Tap
Today they build my Master's tomb

Though I tremble at the sound
would there be an ending to a light eternal?
Sorrow is a page
within the journal
of delight.

Notes

1   Sri Chinmoy, *Twenty-Seven Thousand Aspiration-Plants, Part 4*, Agni Press, 1983, #360

2   Sri Chinmoy, *Two God-Amusement-Rivals: My Heart-Song-Beauty And My Life-Dance-Fragrance, Part 7*, Agni Press, 1996, #693

3   Sri Chinmoy, *The Wings Of Light, Part 15*, Agni Press, 1974, #740

4   Sri Chinmoy, *Three Soulful Prayers*, Agni Press, 1979, #37

5   Sri Chinmoy, *Seventy-Seven Thousand Service-Trees, Part 36*, Agni Press, 2004, #35,781 & #35,782

6   Sri Chinmoy, *The Core Of India's Light, Part 4*, Agni Press, 1992, #57

7   Sri Chinmoy, *Transcendence-Perfection*, Agni Press, 1975, #721

8   Sri Chinmoy, *The Dance Of Life, Part 9*, Agni Press, 1973, #415

9   Sri Chinmoy, *Garden of Love-Light, Part 1*, 1974, Translation of *Tamasa Rate*

10   Sri Chinmoy, *Transcendence-Perfection*, Agni Press, 1975, #716

11   Sri Chinmoy, *Ten Thousand Flower-Flames, Part 25*, Agni Press, 1982, #2,405

12   Sri Chinmoy, *Seventy-Seven Thousand Service-Trees, Part 6*, Agni Press, 1998, #5,771

13   Sri Chinmoy, *Twenty-Seven Thousand Aspiration-Plants, Part 96*, Agni Press, 1984, #9,522

14   Sri Chinmoy, *Twenty-Seven Thousand Aspiration-Plants, Part 133*, Agni Press, 1990, #13,274

15   Sri Chinmoy, *Ten Thousand Flower-Flames, Part 68*, Agni Press, 1983, #6,758

16   Sri Chinmoy, *Seventy-Seven Thousand Service-Trees, Part 36*, Agni Press, 2004, #35,162

17   Sri Chinmoy, *From The Source To The Source*, Agni Press, 1974, #185

18 Sri Chinmoy, *Seventy-Seven Thousand Service-Trees, Part 42*, Agni Press, 2005, #41,252

19 Sri Chinmoy, *Seventy-Seven Thousand Service-Trees, Part 42*, Agni Press, 2005, #41,522

20 Sri Chinmoy, *Seventy-Seven Thousand Service-Trees, Part 42*, Agni Press, 2005, #41,845

21 Sri Chinmoy, *Ten Thousand Flower-Flames, Part 70*, Agni Press, 1983, #6984

About the Author

Sumangali Morhall studied meditation with Indian spiritual Master, Sri Chinmoy, from 1997 until his passing in 2007. English-born, she currently lives in York, UK, where she practices meditation daily, and regularly offers free meditation courses to the public. The name Sumangali (Shoo-mon-go-lee) was given to her by Sri Chinmoy, and means auspicious good fortune.

Websites: www.sumangali.org, www.srichinmoy.org

BOOKS

O is a symbol of the world, of oneness and unity. In different cultures it also means the "eye," symbolizing knowledge and insight. We aim to publish books that are accessible, constructive and that challenge accepted opinion, both that of academia and the "moral majority."

Our books are available in all good English language bookstores worldwide. If you don't see the book on the shelves ask the bookstore to order it for you, quoting the ISBN number and title. Alternatively you can order online (all major online retail sites carry our titles) or contact the distributor in the relevant country, listed on the copyright page.

See our website www.o-books.net for a full list of over 500 titles, growing by 100 a year.

And tune in to myspiritradio.com for our book review radio show, hosted by June-Elleni Laine, where you can listen to the authors discussing their books.

MySpiritRadio